All that we are is the result of what we have thought.
The mind is everything. What we think, we become.

—BUDDHA

ONE BREATH AT A TIME

108 TIMELESS TEACHINGS OF WISDOM

His Holiness
THE DALAI LAMA

ONE BREATH AT A TIME

108 TIMELESS TEACHINGS OF WISDOM

with reflections & meditations
by RAJIV MEHROTRA

HAY HOUSE

HAY HOUSE INDIA
New Delhi • London • Sydney
Carlsbad, California • New York City

Hay House Publishers (India) Pvt Ltd
Muskaan Complex, Plot No. 3, B-2, Vasant Kunj, New Delhi – 110070, India

Hay House LLC, P.O. Box 5100, Carlsbad, CA 92018-5100, USA
Hay House UK Ltd, 1st Floor, Crawford Corner, 91-93 Baker Street, London W1U 6QQ, UK
Hay House Australia Publishing Pty Ltd, 18/36 Ralph St., Alexandria NSW 2015, Australia

Email: contact@hayhouse.co.in
Website: www.hayhouse.co.in

First published by Hay House India, 2025
10 9 8 7 6 5 4 3 2 1

ISBN 978-93-6611-415-6 (Hardback)
ISBN 978-93-6611-163-6 (Ebook)

Printed at Thomson Press

FSC www.fsc.org
MIX
Paper | Supporting responsible forestry
FSC® C010615

Hay House is committed to a sustainable future for our business, our readers and our planet. This book is made from Forest Stewardship Council® certified paper.

To the Dalai Lama at 90

Mountain-born laughter—
a bowl in the rain catches
wisdom without words.

You laughed, and I wept—
not from sorrow, but knowing
what I could become.

Samaya nurtures me—
a thread of light through lifetimes,
grateful beyond speech.

Contents

Introduction 9

How to Use This Book 13

Chapter 1: Foundations of Practice 17
Chapter 2: Mindfulness and Presence 31
Chapter 3: Understanding the Nature of Mind 45
Chapter 4: Working with Difficult Emotions 59
Chapter 5: The Path of Wisdom 73
Chapter 6: Cultivating Compassion 87
Chapter 7: Self-Compassion and Inner Healing 101
Chapter 8: Relationships and Community 115
Chapter 9: Navigating Change and Impermanence 129
Chapter 10: Finding Purpose and Meaning 143
Chapter 11: Ethical Living in Today's World 157
Chapter 12: Joy and Contentment 171
Chapter 13: Meditation Practice 185
Chapter 14: Science and Buddhism 199
Chapter 15: Interfaith Harmony 213
Chapter 16: Environmental Ethics 227
Chapter 17: Integrating Wisdom and Compassion in Daily Life 241
Chapter 18: The Journey of Transformation 255

Glossary of Key Terms with Chapter References 268

Thematic Practice Plans 276

Further Introductory Reading 291

Acknowledgements 295

Introduction

THIS BOOK IS A HUMBLE OFFERING TO MY PRECIOUS GURU and teacher, His Holiness the Fourteenth Dalai Lama, on his ninetieth birthday, July 6th, 2025. For over four decades, I have been blessed to walk, however falteringly, in his radiant shadow. As a student in a relationship of samaya, a seeker, and one among countless others who have turned to him for knowledge and a way of being, I offer these pages as an expression of boundless gratitude.

His Holiness embodies compassion and clarity in a world torn by conflict, uncertainty, and disconnection. He offers not only teachings but presence, not merely answers but a different way of asking the questions that confront our shared human condition.

The 108 quotations in this collection—an auspicious number in Tibetan Buddhist tradition—reflect the breadth and depth of his vision. In Buddhist cosmology and meditative practice, 108 symbolises wholeness. It represents the 108 mental defilements to be overcome on the path to enlightenment or the 108 qualities of the awakened mind. Prayer beads in both Tibetan and Indian traditions often have 108 beads, marking this number as sacred for repetition and reflection. These quotations are offered in that spirit—as a mandala of insight, turning the wheel of compassion and wisdom.

They speak of personal transformation, ethical integrity, interdependence, non-violence, and universal responsibility. Yet quotations alone are like seeds. To take root and bloom, they must be nurtured. That is why each quote is followed by a poetic reflection—an invitation to sit with the insight, to let it speak to the heart—and a meditation prompt, intended as a gentle practice to help integrate the teaching into the rhythms of daily life.His Holiness has a unique way of speaking and writing that often transcends the words. Much of his wisdom is transmitted through presence, through the subtle cadences of his voice, his gestures, and the compassionate energy with which he meets the world. While many polished 'quotable quotes' circulate widely, sparkling in their clarity and often accurately capturing his teachings, they sometimes miss the quiet depth behind his words. In preparing this volume, I have drawn primarily from my own notes and the translations offered by his personal interpreters, hoping to retain the authenticity of his thoughts and the spirit that drives him. These quotations are not strictly verbatim transcriptions; they are curated expressions of his teachings as I have received and understood them over time. I alone bear responsibility for any inaccuracies or misrepresentations.

Throughout his life, the Dalai Lama has emphasised that genuine transformation arises from the union of two essential forces: The penetrating wisdom that sees into the nature of reality and the skilful methods that cultivate positive inner qualities. One without the other is incomplete. The structure of this book reflects that balance through eighteen carefully organised chapters. We begin with foundational practices that open the gateway to inner inquiry, then move through the development of wisdom, the training of the heart-mind, the transformation of afflictive emotions, and the unfolding of compassion. We also explore meditation practices, interfaith harmony, the intersection of science and Buddhism, and environmental ethics. The final chapters integrate these teachings, showing how wisdom and compassion work together in daily life and how to approach the ongoing journey of transformation.

These reflections do not seek to explain or interpret the quotations but rather to feel, to dwell in their presence, as one might sit beside a beloved elder, listening with the whole heart. The meditations are not intended to replace formal instruction or direct transmission from qualified teachers but to offer accessible entry points for readers from all walks of life.

This collection is not only for Buddhists. It is for anyone who aspires to live more gently, think more clearly, and act more lovingly. It is for those who believe, as I do, that wisdom and compassion are not remote ideals but daily choices that shape our humanity.

His Holiness often reminds us that Buddhism is not based on blind faith but on critical inquiry and personal experience. In that spirit, I invite you to approach these pages not as fixed doctrines but as offerings of possibility, open to your own investigation, reflection, and lived engagement. Test these teachings in the laboratory of your mind and heart.

—Rajiv Mehrotra

How to Use This Book

THIS COLLECTION IS MORE THAN A COMPILATION OF quotations—it is an invitation to undertake a gentle, structured journey through the Dalai Lama's integrated path of cultivating wisdom and compassion. Whether approached as a daily ritual, a progressive course of study, or a source of inspiration in times of need, it is designed to meet you where you are.

Preparing to Begin

Choose a quiet time of day—perhaps early morning, before the world has stirred, or evening, when the day begins to settle. Sit in a comfortable and alert posture, with your spine naturally upright, your feet grounded or legs gently crossed, and your hands resting on your lap. Allow your body to be relaxed but attentive.

Take a few conscious breaths. Let the in-breath anchor you in the present; the out-breath releases any tension or distraction. Give yourself permission to pause, to shift inward, and to be with this moment without hurry.

Start with fifteen minutes a day. Using a timer can be very helpful, especially during the early stages of learning to meditate for several practical and psychological reasons: Setting a timer defines a clear beginning and end to the session. This structure helps new practitioners commit to a specific duration, reducing the temptation to repeatedly stop early or check the clock. Without one, beginners may frequently wonder, 'Has it been long enough?' or 'When should I stop?'—distracting themselves from the meditative process. A timer relieves this uncertainty, allowing deeper focus. It encourages discipline by gradually building up your capacity to sit still, especially if you start with short periods (e.g., 5–10 minutes) and increase them over time. Beginners sometimes push too hard, thinking longer sessions are 'better'. A timer can prevent this by setting healthy boundaries and encouraging sustainable growth in attention and stillness. Ironically, using a timer helps you let go of time. You no longer need to mentally calculate how long you've been meditating, allowing you to entirely drop into the present moment.

Let your engagement with the book be part of this sacred pause—an offering to your heart.

Ways to Engage

As a Daily Contemplation

Each morning—or whenever you seek clarity—open the book to a random page. Read the quotation slowly. Let it land. Then, enter the poetic reflection, not to dissect it, but to feel it. If time permits, explore the meditation prompts, even briefly. Carry the essence of what you discover into your day. Let the words become a lens through which you see your experiences afresh.

As a Progressive Study

Move sequentially through the book, as it was carefully structured to unfold like a spiritual journey. Begin with foundational practices that build the inner ground for transformation, then deepen into teachings on wisdom, emotional healing, compassion, and ethical living. Stay with each quotation for a few days. Return to it. Let it sink in before moving to the next. Insight ripens with time.

As a Topical Resource

Use the thematic practice paths at the back of the book to find teachings that speak to your current concerns—whether working with difficult emotions, cultivating compassion, or exploring wisdom. Or refer to the contents page to find chapters addressing specific aspects of the path. Let your need guide your hand. The teachings are not prescriptive but suggestive; they open rather than constrain.

As a Companion to Formal Practice

Read a quotation aloud if you already have a meditation or prayer practice. Let it set the tone for your sitting. Return to it when the mind wanders. Reflect upon it in silence. Let it become the object of your inquiry or the fragrance of your mindfulness. Don't worry if it does—begin again with kindness.

As a Group Study Guide

Gather with friends or fellow seekers. Each week, choose a quotation to sit with in solitude, then meet to share reflections. Use the poetic passages to invite dialogue that touches the heart and explore the meditation exercises together, if possible. Let this be a sangha of shared vulnerability and growth.

Working with the Components

Each entry is composed of four interwoven threads:

1. The Quotation

These are the words of His Holiness, chosen for their clarity and depth. Read them slowly. Let them echo. Observe what opens or resists in you. They are not slogans but signposts—pointing to something to be lived.

2. The Poetic Reflection

These are contemplative, lyrical, and experiential responses in the author's voice. Let them stir your imagination and emotion. Feel into them as you might a piece of music or a memory.

They are not explanations but invitations to intimacy with the teaching.

3. The Meditation Practice

These simple exercises help anchor the teachings in your lived experience. Some are formal meditations; others are mindfulness practices. Even five minutes of sincere engagement can shift your perspective and deepen your understanding.

A Gentle Reminder

The Dalai Lama reminds us that understanding arises not from blind faith but from critical inquiry and personal experience. These teachings are not dogma. They are possibilities. Test them in the laboratory of your own heart and life.

Above all, be patient with yourself. Transformation is not dramatic. It unfolds like the quiet blooming of a lotus—petal by petal, breath by breath. Let each entry meet you gently, like a companion on the path.

Return as often as needed. The teachings are always new because you are constantly changing.

Chapter 1

Foundations of Practice

THIS CHAPTER INTRODUCES THE FUNDAMENTAL PRINCIPLES that form the bedrock of the Dalai Lama's teachings. Like establishing the foundations of a house before building its walls, these core insights provide the stable ground upon which meaningful practice can develop.

The journey of inner transformation begins with understanding our shared human aspiration for happiness and freedom from suffering. This recognition connects us to all other beings and establishes the basis for compassion. We then explore how this transformation occurs not through adding something new to ourselves but by removing the obscurations that hide our innate qualities of clarity and kindness.

The Dalai Lama teaches that our minds operate according to the laws of cause and effect that govern the physical world. Our thoughts, attitudes, and actions create corresponding effects, giving us responsibility for and power over our mental states. This understanding leads to the recognition that genuine happiness emerges not from external circumstances but from systematically training our minds through ethical conduct and consistent practice.

Whether you are new to meditation or a seasoned practitioner, these foundational teachings provide the essential context for the following practices. They remind us that spiritual development is not separate from our ordinary lives but offers a framework for living with greater awareness, integrity, and purpose.

1

Our Shared Aspiration

'Everyone seeks happiness and wishes to avoid suffering. This is not just a human desire but the fundamental nature of all sentient beings. Understanding this universal aspiration creates a natural foundation for compassion.'

Reflection

Our deepest longing,
shared with every living thing—
to find joy, to flee pain.
In this common yearning,
we are never alone.
The thread that binds all life
runs through my heart
and yours.

Meditation

Reflect on how your desire for happiness and freedom from suffering connects you to all living beings. Begin with yourself, acknowledging your natural wish to be happy and pain-free. Next, gradually extend this recognition—first to people you care about, then to acquaintances and strangers, and finally to all living creatures. Observe how this reflection naturally evokes a sense of connection.

2

The Nature of Self-Transformation

'Self-transformation is about changing our thoughts, deeper attitudes, and emotional patterns. This requires honest self-examination and consistent effort over time.'

Reflection

The mirror does not lie,
yet how seldom we truly look.
Beneath the story I tell myself,
what subtle currents flow?
What hidden hands shape
the vessel of my responses?
True change begins
in that brave moment
of unflinching gaze.

Meditation

Choose one reactive pattern you've noticed in yourself, perhaps impatience, self-criticism, or a tendency to worry. When alone, recreate the feeling of being triggered by this pattern, observing the sensations and thoughts that arise with gentle curiosity rather than judgement. Observe where you feel resistance to seeing clearly. What thoughts or beliefs maintain this pattern? What needs might it be trying to meet, however ineffectively?

3

Revealing Our Innate Qualities

'True transformation is not about adding something new but removing the obscurations hiding our innate qualities. Like clearing clouds to reveal the sun, we work to clear away our mental afflictions to reveal our fundamental goodness.'

Reflection

Not in becoming
but in its unveiling.
The masterpiece exists
beneath the dust,
the pure spring
beneath the silt,
the clear sky
behind storm clouds.
We are not empty vessels
waiting to be filled,
but buried treasures
waiting to be found.

Meditation

Sit quietly and imagine your awareness as a clear, open sky. As thoughts and emotions arise, see them as clouds passing through—sometimes light and wispy, occasionally dark and turbulent—but never inherent to the sky itself. Observe how all mental states come and go while the spacious awareness that recognises them remains unchanged. Rest in recognising that clarity and openness are always present, even temporarily obscured.

4

The Law of Cause and Effect

'The law of causality operates in our mental experiences just as it does in the physical world. Negative thoughts and emotions create suffering; positive ones create well-being. By understanding this, we take responsibility for our mental states.'

Reflection

Each thought a seed;
each emotion, the soil;
each action, the water that nourishes.
The harvest of tomorrow
grows from what I plant today.
No divine hand determines
the garden of my experience—
only the humble, consistent work
of tending what I cultivate.

Meditation

Calm your mind and experiment with deliberately cultivating different mental states and observing their effects. First, spend a few minutes dwelling on a minor frustration or worry, noticing how this affects your body, energy, and overall sense of well-being. Then, spend a few minutes cultivating feelings of appreciation or kindness, again, noticing the effects. Compare these experiences. What insights does this give you about the relationship between mental states and well-being?

5

The Nature of Genuine Happiness

'Happiness is not something ready-made.
It comes from training the mind to see reality clearly
and cultivating positive mental states through
consistent practice.'

Reflection

We search for happiness
like a lost object,
looking under rocks and behind trees,
when all along
it emerges from how we look,
not what we find.
The garden of joy
grows not from acquiring
but from cultivating.

Meditation

Investigate the nature of happiness in your own experience. Recall three experiences: When you acquired something you wanted, felt a deep connection with others, and when your mind was clear and at peace. Compare the quality and duration of happiness in each case. Which left you wanting more, and which created a sense of enough? What insights does this give you about the sources of genuine happiness?

6
The Ethical Foundation

'Ethical conduct is the foundation for all spiritual development. Without it, meditation becomes merely a temporary escape rather than a tool for genuine transformation.'

Reflection

The house built on sand
may rise majestically
but cannot withstand the storm.
So, too, the meditations
that float above
the unexamined life.
True refuge comes not from fleeing
but from living with integrity
in each ordinary moment.

Meditation

Reflect on what values are most important to you—such as honesty, kindness, fairness, or courage. For each value, consider how aligning with this value affects my mental well-being and relationships. What happens when my actions contradict this value? Finally, reflect on how ethical conduct creates a foundation of inner harmony that supports deeper spiritual practice.

Chapter 2

Mindfulness and Presence

In a world of constant distraction, practising mindfulness—bringing full awareness to our present experience—offers a revolutionary way of being. Our attention is increasingly fragmented by digital devices, busy schedules, and the relentless stream of information that characterises modern life. The resulting disconnection from direct experience creates a subtle but pervasive form of suffering.

The Dalai Lama teaches that mindfulness serves as both an anchor in the storm of daily life and a gateway to deeper understanding. Unlike some popular approaches that present mindfulness as an end in itself, traditional Buddhist practice views it as a powerful tool that allows us to observe our minds with clarity and develop qualities that lead to genuine happiness.

This chapter explores mindfulness's cultivation through formal meditation and everyday awareness. We investigate how concentration develops through consistent practice, balancing focused attention with analytical inquiry, and recognising and transforming habitual thought patterns before they lead to harmful words or actions.

By learning to drop beneath our endless stream of thoughts into a direct sensory experience, we discover a more immediate and vivid way of relating to life. This presence becomes a respite from digital distraction and a foundation for the wisdom and compassion that naturally unfold when we are fully available to ourselves and others.

7
Mindfulness as a Gateway

'Many people consider mindfulness practice as the goal itself. However, in traditional Buddhist understanding, mindfulness is a foundation that allows us to observe the mind to develop both penetrating wisdom and positive qualities like compassion. It is a gateway, not the destination.'

Reflection

The focused mind,
a well-crafted vessel—
not the water itself,
but that which holds and directs
the flowing current of awareness
towards shores of greater understanding.
Without this vessel,
wisdom spills, uncontained;
compassion dissipates, undirected.

Meditation

Begin with a few minutes of mindful breathing, noticing each breath as it enters and leaves your body. Next, while maintaining this stable attention, introduce the question: 'What is observing these breaths?' Don't grasp for conceptual answers, but allow the question to create a gentle curiosity about the nature of awareness itself. Observe how mindfulness creates a platform for deeper investigation.

8
Developing Concentration

'Concentration develops through consistent practice. Don't be discouraged by distraction! You strengthen your concentration muscles whenever you observe the mind has wandered and bring it back to the object of your attention.'

Reflection

Each return to the breath
is not failure but success—
the moment of awakening
from the dream of distraction.
The wandering is inevitable;
the noticing is the practice.
Like training a puppy,
gentle persistence matters more
than perfect performance.

Meditation

Practise watching and counting each time you observe your mind has wandered and gently bring it back. Rather than being frustrated by the count, recognise each number as a moment of mindfulness and an opportunity to strengthen concentration. At the end, acknowledge the total number of returns with appreciation rather than judgement—each represents a moment of awakening.

9

Direct Experience beyond Concepts

'We are so dominated by thinking that we've become disconnected from direct experience. When we go beyond the conceptual mind, we discover a more immediate and vivid way of relating to life.'

Reflection

The world wrapped in words,
packaged in concepts,
filtered through stories—
this isn't the world at all
but its pale mirror.
Beneath the chatter of thought
lies the realm of direct perception:
the coolness of water on skin,
the play of light on leaves,
the spaciousness of aware presence
that contains all things
in vibrant immediacy.

Meditation

Watch your conceptual thinking for a few minutes, then immerse yourself in a direct sensory experience. Feel the weight and temperature of your body, the texture of sounds around you, the dance of light and colour, the rhythm of your breath—all without naming or analysing. When you observe yourself thinking about or evaluating the experience, gently return to pure sensation. Observe the differencebetween this direct perception and habitual conceptual engagement.

10
Digital Mindfulness

'The constant bombardment of information through digital devices can be a major obstacle to inner peace. While these technologies have benefits, they can prevent us from being fully present. Sometimes, it is necessary to disconnect externally to reconnect internally.'

Reflection

Notifications like hungry ghosts
tug endlessly at our sleeves,
each promising something urgent,
something essential.
Meanwhile, the bird outside our window
sings its complex melody, unheard.
The breath moves in and out, unnoticed.
What treasure might we find
in the space between one thought and the next,
if only we would look?

Meditation

Set aside the session for a 'digital fast'. Turn off all devices or place them in another room. Sit comfortably and simply observe how it feels to be temporarily disconnected—what sensations, emotions, or thoughts arise? Is there restlessness, relief, anxiety, or peace? Watch these responses with gentle curiosity rather than judgement. Before ending, reflect on what this experience reveals about your relationship with technology and presence.

11
Catching Thought Patterns Early

'The essence of mental training is becoming aware of harmful thought patterns as they arise before they can develop into harmful words or actions. This creates the space for conscious choice rather than automatic reaction.'

Reflection

The seedling is easily uprooted,
the spark simply extinguished,
the whisper gently redirected.
But the full-grown tree,
the raging fire,
the shouted word—
these carry a momentum
not easily halted.
Vigilance at the source
spares us the regret of consequences
that cannot be undone.

Meditation

Settle down and practise catching thought patterns at their earliest stages. When you observe a thought arising, label it according to its nature ('planning', 'remembering', 'judging', 'worrying') and observe it without elaboration. Spot the difference between being swept along by thoughts and maintaining awareness of them as they emerge. Pay particular attention to emotionally charged thoughts, noticing how they feel in the body as they arise.

12

Balancing Analysis and Stability

'Analytical meditation investigates the nature of reality, while stabilising meditation develops mental focus. Both are necessary—like a lamp that needs both oil and flame to illuminate the darkness of ignorance.'

Reflection

The steady flame
without direction
merely burns in place.
The searching beam
without focus
scatters its light.
Together they become
the perfect instrument
illuminating what was always there
but hidden from our sight.

Meditation

Divide your meditation session into three parts. First, spend five minutes developing stability by focusing on the breath, allowing the mind to settle. Next, spend five minutes in an analytical mode, investigating a simple question like 'Where exactly is my mind located?' or 'What precisely is experiencing these sensations?' Finally, return to five minutes of stable attention on the breath. Observe the different qualities of these two modes of meditation and how they complement each other.

Chapter 3

Understanding the Nature of Mind

How does our mind create our experience of reality? This profound question lies at the heart of the Dalai Lama's teachings on the nature of the mind. While Western psychology focuses primarily on the content of thoughts and emotions, Buddhist psychology investigates the mind itself—its fundamental nature and how it shapes our experience of the world.

The Dalai Lama draws from Buddhism's sophisticated understanding of the mind to show how our perceptions, thoughts, and emotions shape our reality. This chapter explores the profound insight that much of our suffering stems not from external events but from how our minds interpret and react to them. When we believe our thoughts represent reality precisely as it is, we remain trapped in habitual patterns of reaction and suffering.

Through both analytical meditation and direct observation, we can discover that what we take to be solid, independent realities—including our sense of self—reveal themselves to be more fluid, interdependent, and open to transformation than we had assumed. This understanding doesn't lead to nihilism or meaninglessness but rather to greater freedom and responsibility. When we recognise that our interpretations create our experience, we gain the power to change those interpretations.

As we develop insight into the constructive nature of experience and the interdependence of mind and world, we discover more skilful ways to relate to life's challenges. We learn that beneath our confusion and habitual patterns lies our natural condition of clarity, compassion, and wisdom—qualities not to be added but revealed.

13

The Mind that Constructs Reality

'When we examine our perceptions closely, we discover something startling: Rather than perceiving reality directly, we experience a mental construction shaped by our concepts, language, and past conditioning.'

Reflection

The world I think I see—
solid, separate, permanent—
is more projection than perception.
The mind draws lines
where nature makes none,
creates stories from fragments,
builds walls from whispers.
What freedom might come
from seeing through
these innocent fabrications?

Meditation

Choose an everyday object and examine it closely for some time. First, observe how your mind automatically labels, categorises, and relates to it based on past associations. Then, try to see it freshly, as if encountering it for the first time. Observe the difference between the object as conceptualised and the raw sensory experience of colours, shapes, textures, and weight. Observe how challenging it actually is to perceive without the overlay of concepts.

14
Interpretations and Reality

'Our reactions to life events are shaped more by our interpretations of them than by the events themselves. By changing our perspective, we can transform our experience without changing the external circumstances.'

Reflection

Between stimulus and response
lies the realm of meaning,
the stories we tell,
the assumptions we carry,
the interpretations we construct.
The same rain that ruins one person's plans
saves another's crops.
The criticism that wounds one heart
helps another to grow.
In the space between event and reaction
lives our greatest freedom.

Meditation

Recall a challenging situation from a recent experience. Explore different perspectives on this event. First, write down your initial interpretation and the emotions it generated. Then, deliberately generate three alternative interpretations of the situation—perhaps seeing it as a valuable lesson, an opportunity for growth, or from the other person's perspective. Observe how each interpretation creates a different emotional response and suggests various possible actions.

15
Expectations and Reality

'Much of our suffering comes from comparing our actual experience with our expectations. If we can accept reality as it is, we find a profound peace before applying our concepts of how it should be.'

Reflection

The gap between what is
and what we think should be
this narrow space
generates vast suffering.
The perfect future we construct,
the flawless past we fabricate,
the ideal self we imagine—
all cast shadows on the present moment,
obscuring its own particular beauty,
its own complete sufficiency.

Meditation

Calm your breath, practise alternating between expectation and acceptance. First, bring to mind a situation where reality doesn't match your expectations—perhaps a relationship, work situation, or personal achievement. Observe the feeling of tension or disappointment this creates. Then, practise temporarily setting aside your expectations and meeting your actual experience with acceptance. Observe the shift in your emotional state when you close the gap between expectation and reality. Repeat this process several times in different situations.

16

The Self as Process

'The Buddha did not teach "no-self" as a doctrine to believe, but as a tool for examining our experience. When we look for a permanent, independent self, we cannot find one—only a collection of changing processes.'

Reflection

Searching for the thinker
behind the thoughts,
for the experiencer
behind the experience,
is like looking for the dancer
apart from the dance.
The river flows,
but where is the 'riverness'
apart from flowing water?

Meditation

Relax into the session. Whenever a thought or feeling arises, gently ask, 'Who is thinking this?' or 'Who is feeling this?' Don't settle for the conceptual answer, 'I am,' instead look directly for this 'I' that seems to be at the centre of experience. Is it in the head? The chest? Is it constant or changing? Does it have a shape or location? Observe what you find—or don't find—without rushing to conclusions. The point is not to adopt a belief in 'no-self' but to investigate your direct experience with curiosity.

17

Our Natural Condition

'Our natural condition, beneath our confusion and habitual patterns, is one of clarity, compassion, and wisdom. Spiritual practice adds nothing new but removes the obscurations that hide this innate potential.'

Reflection

The sculptor does not create
the figure in the stone
but reveals what was always there
by removing what is not needed.
So, too, with our awakening—
not becoming something other,
not importing foreign perfection,
but uncovering the luminous nature
that has been present from the beginning,
waiting patiently beneath
the accumulated dust of confusion.

Meditation

Sit quietly and imagine your awareness as the clear blue sky. See thoughts, emotions, and sensations as clouds pass through this sky—some light and wispy, others dark and turbulent. Observe that no matter how many clouds appear, the sky itself remains unaffected, spacious, and clear. Rest in the recognition that this basic awareness—clear, spacious, and knowing—is your natural condition. When you get caught in a particular cloud (thought or emotion), gently return to the perspective of the sky.

18

Inner Discipline and Freedom

'Inner discipline is the basis of a good and happy life. This doesn't mean a stiff, militaristic discipline imposed from outside. Rather, the self-discipline comes from recognising that your actions have consequences, not just for others but for your own state of mind.'

Reflection

What binds us is not the rope around our wrists
but the thoughts we refuse to examine.
Freedom grows not from the absence of constraints
but presence of awareness—
the quiet recognition that each moment of choice
shapes who we become.

Meditation

Reflect on the relationship between discipline and freedom in your life. First, identify areas where a lack of discipline (acting on every impulse) actually limits your freedom by creating negative consequences. Then, identify areas where self-discipline (mindful choice) has expanded your freedom by creating favourable conditions in your life and mind. Consider how conscious choice—rather than automatic habit—represents true freedom.

Chapter 4

Working with Difficult Emotions

EMOTIONS LIKE ANGER, FEAR, ATTACHMENT, AND JEALOUSY ARE often seen as obstacles on the spiritual path. Yet the Dalai Lama offers a more nuanced perspective: Difficult emotions are not enemies to be suppressed, nor should they be unthinkingly expressed. Instead, he offers a middle way—meeting these emotions with awareness and understanding their deeper causes.

This approach differs significantly from Western and Eastern misconceptions. While some Western approaches might encourage uninhibited emotional expression, and some Eastern traditions seem to advocate suppression, the Buddhist approach is more subtle. It recognises that emotions are valuable but can be problematic when they overwhelm our awareness and drive reactive behaviour.

This chapter explores practical approaches to transforming difficult emotions through mindfulness, insight, and specific antidotes. We learn to create space around our emotional reactions, understand their underlying causes, and redirect our energy constructively. Rather than treating emotions as personal failings to overcome, we approach them with curiosity and compassion—as natural human experiences that, when understood, can become doorways to greater freedom and wisdom.

The Dalai Lama teaches that even anger, often considered the most destructive emotion, contains energy that can be harnessed for positive change when separated from hostile intentions. Fear, too, often reveals itself as a misguided protector, trying to keep us safe but limiting our growth. By neither suppressing nor indulging these emotions but meeting them with mindful awareness, we discover the possibility of emotional freedom—not freedom from emotions, but freedom in how we relate to them.

19
Beyond Suppression and Indulgence

'Simply suppressing or denying negative emotions never works in the long term. Instead, we must understand their causes and transform their energy through awareness and applying appropriate antidotes.'

Reflection

The closed door
contains what's behind it
but does not make it disappear.
The buried seed
does not cease to exist
but grows in darkness
until it breaks through,
often where least expected.
Better to bring all into light—
not to indulge or condemn,
but to understand and transform.

Meditation

When a complex emotion arises during this practice (or recall one from recent experience), work with it. Acknowledge its presence without suppression. Name it ('This is anger' or 'This is fear') and observe where and how you feel it in your body. Investigate its causes and triggers with kindness. What thoughts or situations feed this emotion? What unmet need or threatened value might lie beneath it? Apply a specific antidote: For anger, cultivate patience; for hatred, develop compassion; for attachment, contemplate impermanence. Observe how different this approach feels from your habitual ways of handling emotions.

20
Understanding Anger

'When we examine anger closely,
we find it comes from feeling threatened.
This threat may be to our physical safety, but
more often to our self-image or cherished beliefs.
Understanding this helps us respond more skilfully.'

Reflection

The flaring match
reveals not just its own fire
but the hidden places
where we feel small, unheard, unseen.
Behind the clenched fist,
a frightened heart protects
its vulnerable centre.
What wisdom might come
if before rushing to battle,
we first inquired within:
'What part of me feels threatened?'

Meditation

Explore the roots of anger in your experience. Recall a recent situation where you felt angry, even if mildly. Rather than re-experiencing the whole emotion, maintain a witnessing awareness as you investigate: What exactly felt threatened? Was it your physical safety, self-image, values, or sense of control? Observe how identifying the specific threat changes your relationship to the anger and opens new possibilities for responding.

21
The Transformative Power of Awareness

'The key to transforming negative emotions is mindful awareness, not suppression or indulgence. By clearly observing anger or desire, we create space around it and discover the freedom to respond skilfully.'

Reflection

Neither pushing away
nor being swept along,
but standing at the riverbank
watching the current rush by.
This is the narrow path
between denial and drowning,
the art of transformation
that turns turbulent waters
into nourishing rain.

Meditation

Practise observing the mind for whatever emotions arise. If no strong emotion is present, work with a mild one or recall a recent emotional experience. Recognise the emotion without judgement ('This is frustration'). Accept its presence without trying to change it. Investigate it with curiosity—observe its physical sensations, the thoughts feeding it, and how it changes moment by moment. Non-identification—observe how the emotion is an experience passing through awareness, not a permanent part of who you are. Observe how this approach differs from being completely identified with the emotion or trying to push it away.

22

True Power Versus Reactive Anger

'Anger may appear powerful, but it actually weakens us by clouding judgement and blocking access to our deeper wisdom. The truly powerful response comes from clarity and compassion.'

Reflection

The storm seems mighty
as it uproots trees and floods valleys,
yet resolves nothing,
creates nothing,
leaves only recovery in its wake.
The gentle persistence of water
shapes mountains,
creates canyons,
nourishes life.
True power lies not in destruction
but in the transforming patience
that creates new possibilities.

Meditation

Compare two approaches to addressing a challenging situation in your life. First, imagine responding with reactive anger—visualise how this would feel in your body, what you might say or do, and what consequences might follow. Then, imagine facing the same situation with clarity and compassion—how would this feel differently in your body? What actions might arise? What different outcomes might be possible? Observe which response gives you more genuine influence and which aligns better with your deeper values.

23

Harnessing the Energy of Anger

'Anger is not inherently destructive.
When understood and channelled properly, its energy can fuel positive action. The key is to separate the energy of anger from the hostile intention that typically accompanies it.'

Reflection

The same fire that burns down forests
also cooks meals and warms homes.
The same current that causes shock
also powers lights and healing machines.
So, too, with anger's powerful energy—
destructive when unleashed blindly,
transformative when harnessed with wisdom,
illuminating what must change
without consuming the heart that feels it.

Meditation

Practise separating the components of anger. The raw energy—Observe the physical sensations of intensity, heat, or power in the body. The underlying caring—Identify what value or boundary has been violated. The hostile intention—Observe any thoughts of harm or revenge. Channel the energy towards constructive protection of what you value, without the hostile element. Visualise this energy fuelling clear communication, appropriate boundary-setting, or committed action rather than aggression.

24

Working with Fear

'Fear often masquerades as wisdom, cautioning us against taking risks or opening our hearts. Through Buddhist practice, we learn to distinguish between reasonable caution and the habitual fears that limit our potential for growth and connection.'

Reflection

The voice of fear speaks
in reasonable tones,
disguised as prudence,
camouflaged as wisdom.
'Better safe,' it whispers,
'better closed than vulnerable.'
Yet the unopened hand
can neither give nor receive.
The unplanted seed
never knows what it might become.

Meditation

Examine fear closely. Identify a specific fear in your life, perhaps fear of failure, rejection, change, or vulnerability. Observe the physical sensations of fear in your body. Listen to fear's 'story'—what does it explicitly predict will happen? Investigate this prediction with gentle questioning: 'Is this certainly true? What evidence supports or contradicts this belief? What's the worst that could truly occur, and could I handle it if it did?' Observe how this rational inquiry affects the emotional intensity of the fear.

Chapter 5

The Path of Wisdom

Wisdom in the Buddhist tradition goes far beyond intellectual knowledge—a profound understanding of the nature of reality transforms how we perceive ourselves and our world. Where knowledge accumulates information, wisdom penetrates beneath appearances to discern the fundamental nature of things. This wisdom is not abstract philosophy but a practical insight that liberates us from confusion and suffering.

The Dalai Lama teaches that cultivating wisdom is essential for genuine happiness. Without it, even our compassion remains incomplete—like trying to help someone find their way through unfamiliar terrain without a map. The key insights that constitute wisdom concern the true nature of reality: That all phenomena are interdependent rather than independent, impermanent rather than permanent, and empty of inherent existence rather than solidly real in the way they appear.

This chapter explores these profound insights through both conceptual understanding and contemplative practice. We begin by investigating interdependence—how everything exists in relation to innumerable causes and conditions. We then examine the nature of 'emptiness' (śūnyatā), perhaps the most misunderstood concept in Buddhism. Far from nihilism, emptiness points to the open, interdependent nature of reality that is fuller and richer than our conceptual projections.

As our understanding deepens, we discover that wisdom is not something outside ourselves to be acquired, but a natural capacity that emerges as we clear away our confused ways of seeing. This wisdom becomes the foundation for a more spacious, compassionate way of being in the world.

25

The Web of Interdependence

'Interdependence means that nothing exists in isolation. Every person, object, and event arises through countless causes and conditions and exists only in relation to everything else.'

Reflection

This cup before me—
clay shaped by human hands,
fired in kilns built by others,
filled with water purified
by both nature and technology,
brought to my lips
by arm and hand
nourished through a vast web
of agriculture and commerce.
What appears simple
contains the whole world.

Meditation

Choose any object you use daily and spend fifteen minutes tracing back all the elements that had to come together for it to exist—materials, people, knowledge, transportation systems, energy sources. Extend this web of connections as far as possible, noting how even the simplest item connects you to countless beings and processes across time and space. Then reflect: How does this understanding of interdependence change your relationship to this object and the world that produced it?

26
The Rainbow of Emptiness

'The concept of emptiness doesn't mean things don't exist, but that they exist interdependently, without fixed, inherent existence. Like a rainbow that appears through the coming together of light, water, and an observer.'

Reflection

The rainbow arches
across the valley—
unmistakably present
yet impossible to grasp.
Try to find its edge,
its beginning or end,
its location in space,
and it dissolves into relations:
Light meeting water meeting eye.
Not less real for being empty,
but more wondrous in its
dependent arising.

Meditation

Contemplate the nature of a rainbow as a metaphor for emptiness. Visualise a rainbow appearing after a rainstorm—vividly present yet formed entirely through the relationships between sunlight, water droplets, and your perspective as the observer. If any of these elements were missing, the rainbow would not appear. Consider how the rainbow exists—neither as a solid, independent object nor a complete illusion, but as an appearance arising from causes and conditions. Then, apply this understanding to other phenomena in your experience—your body, emotions, relationships, and sense of self.

27
Solidity as Illusion

'What appears solid and independent—whether a physical object or our sense of self—reveals itself upon analysis to be interdependent, transient, and ungraspable. This is not nihilism, but the discovery of a more profound reality.'

Reflection

The wave rises, convinced
of its separate existence,
proud of its unique form,
until that moment of realisation:
There is no wave apart from water,
no fixed self apart from the flowing process.
Not loss but expansion—
the drop rediscovering
it has always been an ocean.

Meditation

Choose an object that seems very solid and permanent. For fifteen minutes, examine it closely while reflecting on three aspects of its nature. (1) Interdependence: How it depends on countless conditions for its existence. (2) Impermanence: How it is constantly changing at the microscopic levels. (3) Emptiness: How it lacks any permanent essence that exists independently of conditions. Observe how this analysis shifts your perception of its seemingly solid nature. Does this understanding diminish the object's reality or enrich your appreciation of its complex existence?

28

Looking for the Essence

'To understand the emptiness of inherent existence, we must scrutinise phenomena. When we look for the essence of anything—a table, a person, even our own mind—we find only interdependent parts and processes, never a fixed, independent core.'

Reflection

The table—where exactly is it?
In the flat surface? The supporting legs?
The atoms comprising both?
The concept in the designer's mind?
The function it serves?
The harder we search for its essence,
the more it dissolves into relations,
perspectives, temporary assemblages.
Not non-existent,
but existing in dependence,
like every other phenomenon
including ourselves.

Meditation

Investigate your sense of self through analytical meditation. Examine your body—can you identify the essential 'you'? Is it your brain, heart, or the sum of all parts? Explore your mind—is there a thinker separate from thoughts, a feeler from feelings, an observer from observations? Consider your sense of continuity—how has 'you' changed from childhood to now, and what remains the same? Experience the open question of identity without trying to reach a fixed conclusion or replace one view with another. Observe how this investigation affects your sense of self.

29

Beyond Concepts

'Concepts cannot capture ultimate reality. Yet we use concepts as tools to point towards that which is beyond conception, like using a thorn to remove a thorn before discarding both.'

Reflection

Words about water
cannot quench thirst.
Maps of mountains
cannot provide the view.
Yet without the map,
how would we find our way?
We build a raft to cross the river,
not to carry on our backs
once we reach the other shore.

Meditation

Select a meaningful word or concept (like 'love', 'awareness', or 'freedom'). Work with it for fifteen minutes. Reflect on the concept deeply—what does it mean? What experiences does it point to? Set aside the concept and try to experience directly what it points to beyond the label and definition. Observe the difference between conceptual understanding and direct experience. Recognise how concepts serve as useful tools while acknowledging their limitations in capturing reality directly.

30

Levels of Understanding

'In Buddhist epistemology, we recognise different levels of understanding: Received knowledge from trusted sources, inferential understanding through reasoning, and direct perception through sustained contemplation. Each level takes us closer to the truth.'

Reflection

First, the map handed down
by those who travelled before us.
Then, our own careful footsteps
testing the terrain,
connecting landmark to landmark
through the thread of logic.
Finally, the moment when the mountain
reveals itself directly,
no longer a concept or conclusion
but the ground beneath our feet.

Meditation

Choose a teaching that resonates with you (like impermanence or compassion. Received knowledge: Recall what you've learnt about this teaching from others. Appreciate the value of this transmitted wisdom. Inferential understanding: Examine it through logical reasoning. What evidence supports it? How does it connect with other truths you've verified? Direct perception: Look for ways to observe it directly in your immediate experience, beyond concepts and reasoning. Observe the different qualities of understanding at each level and how they complement one another.

Chapter 6

Cultivating Compassion

COMPASSION—THE GENUINE WISH FOR OTHERS TO BE FREE from suffering—stands at the heart of the Dalai Lama's teachings and personal example. Often described as the essence of spiritual practice, compassion is not merely a sentimental emotion but a robust response to the reality of suffering that combines warm-heartedness with clear insight and courageous action.

The Dalai Lama distinguishes between emotional sympathy, which fluctuates based on our feelings towards others, and genuine compassion, which remains stable because it's grounded in recognising our shared humanity. Where sympathy may lead to emotional burnout or selective concern, compassion provides a sustainable foundation for genuine care that extends to all beings, regardless of our personal connection to them.

This chapter explores how compassion can be systematically cultivated through understanding our shared human experience and applying specific practices. We begin by recognising that all beings wish for happiness and freedom from suffering, just as we do ourselves. This common ground creates the basis for genuine concern that transcends the usual boundaries of close and distant relationships.

Here, we explore how compassion benefits not only its recipients but also becomes the source of our own most profound happiness and meaning. As the Dalai Lama often emphasises, if you want others to be happy, practise compassion; if you want yourself to be happy, practise compassion.

Perhaps, most profoundly, we discover that compassion and wisdom are inseparable. When we genuinely understand the interdependent nature of reality, we recognise that others' well-being is inseparable from our own. This insight transforms compassion from a deliberate practice to a natural expression of our most precise understanding.

31
The Common Ground of Compassion

'Genuine compassion is based on the recognition that others, just like me, naturally want happiness and do not want suffering. Upon this recognition, we develop concern for their well-being.'

Reflection

Beneath all our differences—
language, culture, belief—
lies this common ground:
The wish to flourish,
the wish to be free from pain.
When I truly see this sameness,
the stranger becomes familiar,
the boundary begins to blur,
and your well-being
becomes as natural a concern
as my own.

Meditation

Cultivate compassion through recognising our shared humanity. Begin by connecting with your natural desire for happiness and freedom from suffering. Feel this wish in your heart. Bring to mind someone you love, recognising they share this same wish. Extend your genuine concern for their well-being to an acquaintance, then a stranger, and eventually someone difficult, acknowledging their fundamental desire for happiness, just like yours. Notice any resistance that arises as you expand the circle and gently return to the recognition of our common humanity.

32
Stable Compassion beyond Sympathy

'Genuine compassion is not based on our subjective feelings towards others but on recognising their fundamental right to be happy and free from suffering, just like ourselves. This makes it much more stable than emotional sympathy.'

Reflection

Beyond the fluctuating tides
of like and dislike,
beyond the selective concern
that embraces some while excluding others,
lies the steady ground of recognition:
This being before me
shares the same essential wish
as beats within my own heart.
Not a sentiment that comes and goes,
but a truth that remains
when clearly seen.

Meditation

Bring to mind someone towards whom you naturally feel emotional sympathy. Observe the warm, connected feeling this evokes and its potentially fluctuating nature. How might this feeling change if the person's behaviour or appearance changed? Then shift to recognition-based compassion: Regardless of your emotional connection, acknowledge this person's fundamental right to happiness and freedom from suffering—a right identical to your own. Observe the more stable, principled quality of this perspective. Practise this same shift with people towards whom you feel neutral or even adverse, observing how recognition-based compassion can extend where emotional sympathy might not naturally reach.

33
Compassion with Wisdom

'Our view of compassion is often too sentimental. True compassion includes warmth and wisdom—the courage to witness suffering and the wisdom to respond skilfully rather than reactively.'

Reflection

Compassion wears not only
the gentle face of mercy,
but also the fierce countenance
of protective action.
Sometimes, it speaks in whispers,
sometimes, in thunderous challenge.
It knows when to comfort,
when to confront,
when to simply witness.
Its task is not to please
but to truly serve.

Meditation

Bring to mind a situation where someone is suffering—perhaps a personal relationship or a social issue you care about. First, connect with the heart of compassion—the genuine wish to relieve this suffering. Feel this wish as a warm, caring energy in your heart. Then, engage the wisdom aspect: What causes and conditions create this suffering? What response would address these causes rather than just temporarily alleviating symptoms? What unintended consequences might even well-intentioned help create? Observe how this balanced approach—warm-hearted but clear-seeing—differs from either cold analysis or emotional reactivity alone.

34
Expanding the Circle of Concern

'Developing universal compassion begins with recognising that all beings have been our mothers in previous lives, caring for us with the same tenderness that our mother showed in this life. This may seem strange, but it's a powerful method for expanding our circle of concern.'

Reflection

If endless lives stretch behind me,
then each being I meet
has played every role:
Mother, father, child, friend,
enemy, stranger, teacher.
The man who cuts me off in traffic,
the woman begging on the corner—
in some forgotten time,
they may have given their lives for mine.
How then shall I regard them now?

Meditation

Practise expanding your circle of concern through visualisation. If the traditional Buddhist concept of past lives resonates with you, contemplate how, in the vastness of time, every being has at some point been your mother, caring for you with love and kindness. If this approach doesn't resonate, consider how someone has nurtured every person, known love, and has the capacity for kindness—just like you. Think of someone you find difficult. Imagine them as someone who cared for you in a past life, or as someone who has been cared for and shown care themselves. Visualise how they might have demonstrated love and sacrifice. Notice how this perspective changes your feelings towards them now.

35
The Practice of Tonglen

'The practice of tonglen—taking in others' suffering and sending out relief—demonstrates the transformative power of compassion. Instead of avoiding others' pain, we willingly connect with it, discovering that this very connection transforms both ourselves and others.'

Reflection

The instinct to turn away,
to shield the heart from pain,
seems protective but becomes a prison.
The counterintuitive movement
of turning towards suffering,
breathing in the heavy darkness,
breathing out light and relief,
reveals a paradoxical truth:
What we dare to fully face
loses power to imprison us,
and what we embrace with compassion
becomes the path to freedom.

Meditation

Sit comfortably and take several natural breaths to centre yourself. As you inhale, visualise drawing in the suffering of a specific person or group as a dark cloud. Instead of rejecting it, embrace it with the wish to alleviate their pain. As you exhale, visualise sending light, relief, and healing to them—offering what would bring them happiness and well-being. If the visualisation feels difficult, you can simply align the wish to take away suffering with your in-breath and the wish to give happiness with your out-breath. Continue this rhythm, noticing how it challenges our tendency to avoid others' pain and hoard our own happiness.

36

Compassion and Emptiness

'When we truly understand emptiness—the lack of inherent, independent existence in all phenomena—compassion arises naturally. Seeing that all beings exist interdependently, their suffering and well-being become inseparable from our own.'

Reflection

The hand does not ask
if the finger's pain is its concern.
The parent does not calculate
whether the child's hunger matters.
When boundaries dissolve
not through forced obligation
but through clear perception
of our interwoven reality,
care for others becomes as natural
as protecting our own body,
as breathing itself.

Meditation

Explore the relationship between wisdom and compassion by contemplating the countless ways your existence depends on others, from those who grow your food and build your shelter to those who taught you language and skills. Extend this reflection to include how your actions affect others, creating conditions for their suffering or well-being. Consider: If we truly exist interdependently, what happens to the sharp boundary between 'my suffering' and 'your suffering'? Between 'my happiness' and 'your happiness'? Observe how this recognition of interdependence naturally evokes a sense of care and responsibility for others' welfare that doesn't need to be forced or manufactured.

Chapter 7

Self-Compassion and Inner Healing

WHILE COMPASSION FOR OTHERS IS ESSENTIAL, THE Dalai Lama teaches that genuine care must begin with oneself. This perspective may seem surprising coming from a tradition often associated with selflessness. Still, it reflects a profound understanding: We cannot sustainably offer to others what we haven't cultivated within.

Self-compassion is frequently misunderstood in both Eastern and Western contexts. It is not self-indulgence, narcissism, or making excuses for harmful behaviour. Instead, it means bringing the same qualities of kindness, understanding, and wisdom to our own struggles that we would offer to a dear friend. It involves acknowledging our humanity, including our imperfections and mistakes, without harsh judgement or denial.

This chapter explores practices that foster self-compassion, helping us heal inner wounds and develop a healthier relationship with ourselves. We begin with the foundation—recognising that self-compassion creates the necessary reservoir from which compassion for others naturally flows. We then explore how to work skilfully with external and internal criticism, seeing it as potential material for growth rather than an occasion for self-condemnation.

Forgiveness, both of others and ourselves, is essential for inner healing. The Dalai Lama teaches that true forgiveness involves freeing ourselves from resentment, which harms us more than those who wronged us. Self-forgiveness means taking responsibility without letting shame hinder our growth. From this inner kindness, our ability to care for others expands naturally, reflecting our true selves.

37
The Foundation of Compassion

'Self-compassion is the foundation for compassion towards others. If we cannot meet our own suffering with kindness, our compassion for others will be limited and eventually exhausted.'

Reflection

The well that runs dry
can offer no water to the thirsty.
The lamp without oil
cannot illuminate the darkness.
The heart that hardens against itself
builds walls that keep all others out.
The gentle hand we extend inward
becomes the same hand
that reaches outward with authentic care.

Meditation

Bring awareness to an area of struggle, disappointment, or pain in your life—something that typically evokes self-criticism or shame. Observe your habitual response to this difficulty. Is there judgement, denial, or harshness in how you relate to this aspect of your experience? Then, imagine how you would respond if a dear friend shared this same struggle with you. What tone of voice would you use? What words might you offer? What understanding or perspective might you bring? Gently turn this same quality of kind attention towards yourself. You might place a hand on your heart and offer words of understanding: 'This is difficult. This is part of being human. May I be kind to myself in this struggle.' Observe any resistance to this self-compassion and acknowledge it without judgement.

38

Learning from Criticism

'When someone criticises you, practise investigating whether there is truth in their words rather than automatically defending yourself. This open, honest self-examination is the foundation of genuine growth.'

Reflection

The messenger at the gate
brings news we'd rather not hear.
How easy to shoot this messenger,
to bar the unwelcome words,
to fortify the walls of self-defence.
Yet what treasure might we find
by opening that gate with curiosity,
receiving even difficult truths
as potential gifts,
as mirrors revealing
what we cannot see from within?

Meditation

Recall the criticism and noticing your immediate emotional response. Allow these feelings to be present without judgement. Then, with as much objectivity as you can manage, extract the core content of the criticism from the delivery. Setting aside how it was said or who said it, ask yourself with genuine curiosity: 'Is there any truth here that could help me grow?' If you find some truth, acknowledge it without harsh self-judgement. If you don't, reflect on why someone might have this perception, even if it doesn't match your self-understanding. Observe the difference between this approach and your habitual reaction to criticism, whether that's defensive rejection or uncritical acceptance.

39
True Forgiveness

'Genuine forgiveness comes not from suppressing anger but from understanding its causes and the suffering behind harmful actions. This understanding naturally dissolves resentment, leaving clarity and compassion.'

Reflection

True forgiveness arises
not from gritted teeth
and forced amnesia,
but from the clear seeing
that transforms perception.
The one who harmed
appears not as a monster
but as a fellow traveller,
caught in their own tangle
of pain and confusion.
The heart opens not on command
but through insight's gentle unfurling.

Meditation

Think of someone who has hurt you moderately—not your deepest wound, but significant enough to address. First, acknowledge the pain: 'This hurt. This matters.' Next, objectively consider what might have led this person to act harmfully—their suffering, misperceptions, and past influences. This is not to excuse their behaviour, but to understand it in context. See if this broader perspective softens your feelings towards them. If not, that's alright—genuine forgiveness cannot be forced, but arises naturally from understanding.

40
Releasing the Coal of Resentment

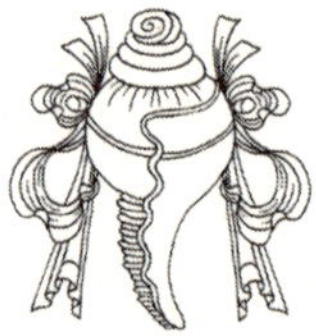

'Forgiveness doesn't mean you excuse harmful actions. It means you choose to release the burning coal of anger and resentment that harms you more than the person who wronged you.'

Reflection

The ledger of wrongs,
carefully maintained,
becomes its own prison.
Each grievance, a brick
in the wall that surrounds
my own heart.
Forgiveness is not
weakness or amnesia,
but the quiet strength
that sets down the burden
I never needed to carry.

Meditation

Bring to mind someone towards whom you hold resentment. Observe where and how this resentment manifests in your body—tension, heat, or heaviness. Visualise this resentment as a burning coal that you've been holding in your hand. Feel its heat, weight, and how it harms you while not affecting the person who hurt you. Explore what it would feel like to set down this coal—not for the other person's sake, but for your freedom. What fears or objections arise at the thought of letting go? What would become possible if you weren't carrying this weight? Imagine opening your hand and releasing the coal, feeling the relief as your hand cools and recovers.

41

Self-Awareness in Virtue

'Even virtuous motivations benefit from examination. Sometimes what appears as generosity conceals a subtle desire for recognition, or what seems like compassion masks a sense of superiority. Genuine virtue comes with self-awareness.'

Reflection

The gift given with fanfare,
the praise expected in return,
the subtle sense of being better
for having been generous—
how these infiltrate even
our noblest intentions.
Not to condemn but to clarify,
we shine the light inward,
separating genuine gold
from its convincing imitations.

Meditation

Recall a recent action you took with good intentions—perhaps helping someone, making a donation, or offering advice. Examine what other motivations might have been present alongside your virtuous intent with gentle curiosity rather than harsh judgement. Were there desires for recognition, approval, or reciprocation? Was there a subtle feeling of superiority or a need to be seen as 'good'? Observe how this awareness of mixed motivations doesn't diminish your good action but rather creates the possibility for even more authentic virtue in the future. Reflect on how genuine virtue naturally emerges as we become more aware of and less driven by our subtle self-centred motivations.

42
The Practice of Gratitude

'Gratitude is a profound practice that counters our tendency towards dissatisfaction. By appreciating what we have—especially our human life with its potential for awakening—we find contentment that no external acquisition could provide.'

Reflection

The eyes that see,
the ears that hear,
the heart that beats unbidden,
the mind that comprehends these words—
such everyday miracles
pass unnoticed in the rush
for more, for different, for better.
Yet when truly seen,
even ordinary bread and water
become a feast beyond measure,
and this imperfect life
reveals itself as precious beyond compare.

Meditation

Begin with the basics—your body and its functioning. Appreciate your breath, senses, beating heart, and the miracle of consciousness itself. Then, consider the conditions that support your life—shelter, food, clean water, and the countless people and systems that provide these necessities. Acknowledge the relationships that nurture you, even brief encounters that have shaped your journey. Finally, appreciate the opportunity for inner development that this human life provides—the capacity for awareness, growth, compassion, and wisdom. Observe how this grateful recognition shifts your perspective from what's missing to what's already abundantly present.

Chapter 8

Relationships and Community

OUR CONNECTIONS WITH OTHERS FORM THE FABRIC OF OUR lives, providing our greatest joys and significant challenges. The quality of our relationships directly impacts our happiness and well-being. Yet, many receive little guidance on cultivating healthy, meaningful connections with family, friends, colleagues, and the wider community.

The Dalai Lama emphasises transforming relationships through understanding, dialogue, and genuine respect for differences, highlighting the equality of all beings and their right to happiness. This perspective shifts relationships from transactions to opportunities for mutual growth and shared well-being.

This chapter explores the vital distinction between genuine love and attachment—a difference that radically transforms how we relate to others. Where attachment focuses on how others make us feel or what they provide, authentic love wishes for their happiness, regardless of what we receive in return. This understanding frees relationships from the burden of meeting all our needs. It creates space for others to flourish as they truly are.

We then explore the four qualities that constitute what Buddhism calls 'true love': Loving-kindness (the wish for others' happiness), compassion (the wish for them to be free from suffering), appreciative joy (celebrating their good fortune), and equanimity (maintaining steady love regardless of circumstances). These four qualities create relationships marked by warmth and wisdom when developed together.

The Dalai Lama teaches that dialogue across differences—whether interpersonal or intercultural—begins with the willingness to listen deeply before being heard. This approach transforms potential conflicts into opportunities for greater understanding and connection.

43
The Quality of Relationships

'The quality of our relationships directly impacts our happiness. But lasting relationships aren't built on mere attachment or need, but on genuine respect and concern for the other's well-being.'

Reflection

Two trees growing side by side
may intertwine their branches,
but their roots remain separate,
drawing nourishment
from their own depths.
So, too, with love
that honours separateness
while celebrating connection.

Meditation

Consider an essential relationship in your life. Bring this person to mind with a sense of appreciation for who they truly are, beyond what they provide for you. Reflect on the difference between moments when you've related from need or attachment versus moments of genuine respect and care for that person's independent well-being. How does each approach feel in your body? What quality of connection results? Contemplate how respecting the other's separate journey—their right to make choices and grow in their own way—paradoxically creates the conditions for genuine closeness. Visualise this relationship as two strong trees growing side by side—connected but not dependent, supporting each other without diminishing either's unique nature.

44
Love Versus Attachment

'Attachment is often confused with love, but they are fundamentally different. Love wishes for the other's happiness while attachment focuses on what we can get from them to secure our own happiness.'

Reflection

Love holds with open palms;
attachment grasps with tight fingers.
Love celebrates the flight;
attachment clips the wings.
Love offers freedom to grow;
attachment demands guarantees.
One expands the heart;
the other contracts it
into anxious vigilance.

Meditation

Think of someone you care about deeply. With honest self-examination, observe where genuine love and attachment might coexist in your feelings towards them. Identify elements of genuine love—wishing for their happiness regardless of what you receive, taking joy in their freedom and growth, wanting what's truly best for them even if it doesn't involve you. Also observe elements of attachment—needing them to be a certain way for your security or satisfaction, feeling threatened by their independence, or having your well-being depend on their responses to you. Feel how these attitudes manifest in your body and mind. Where does love bring spaciousness and warmth? Where does attachment cause tension and anxiety? Gradually shift from the constricted feeling of attachment to the open, generous nature of love.

45
The Four Qualities of True Love

'True love includes four elements: Loving-kindness, the wish for others to have happiness; compassion, the wish for others to be free from suffering; appreciative joy, rejoicing in others' happiness; and equanimity, remaining steady in love regardless of the other's response.'

Reflection

The whole symphony of love
plays all movements:
The gentle melody of kindness,
offering happiness without condition.
The resonant chord of compassion,
responding to pain with care.
The bright allegro of appreciative joy,
celebrating others' good fortune.
The steady bass of equanimity,
maintaining balance through all variations.
Together, they create
the complete music of the heart.

Meditation

Begin with loving-kindness—wish for this person's happiness. Visualise them thriving with, 'May you be happy. May you be well. May your life be filled with joy.' Move to compassion—acknowledge their struggles: 'May you be free from suffering. May your difficulties ease. May you find peace.' Develop appreciative joy—celebrate their successes without comparison: 'May your happiness continue. May your good fortune increase. May your positive qualities flourish.' Finally, cultivate equanimity—recognise their happiness is their own journey: 'Though I care deeply for you, your path is yours. I offer my love regardless.'"

46

Relating to Difficult People

'When dealing with difficult people, remember that negative behaviours are not the person but rather symptoms of their suffering. This perspective helps us respond with compassion rather than reactive hostility.'

Reflection

The thorny exterior
often protects the most tender heart.
The porcupine's quills,
the turtle's shell,
the human's harsh words—
all defences against vulnerability,
signals of past wounds,
armour donned in a world
that felt unsafe.
Seeing beyond the barrier
to the being behind it
transforms both observer and observed.

Meditation

Think of someone whose behaviour you find challenging. Visualise them clearly, acknowledging the genuine difficulties they create. Then, with curiosity rather than judgement, imagine what pain or fear might be driving their actions. What might their difficult behaviour be protecting? What unmet needs might it express? Without excusing harmful actions, practise seeing the vulnerable human being behind the behaviour—someone who, like you, wishes to be happy and free from suffering but may be caught in unskilful patterns. Send healing wishes: 'May your suffering be eased and may you find better ways to meet your needs.' Notice how this changes your emotional response.

47
Understanding the Roots of Harmful Behaviour

'In dealing with difficult people, remember that their harmful behaviour arises from their own suffering and confused thinking. This doesn't excuse their actions but helps us respond with composure rather than escalating hostility.'

Reflection

Behind the harsh words,
a heart constricted by fear.
Behind the harmful actions,
a mind clouded by confusion.
Like a person thrashing in quicksand,
causing danger to rescuers
through their own panic.
Understanding this
doesn't remove the challenge
but transforms how we meet it—
with steadiness that serves
both them and us.

Meditation

Consider a recent situation where someone acted harmfully or unskilfully towards you or others. First, acknowledge the impact of their actions without minimising or exaggerating. Then, with as much objectivity as possible, consider what conditions might have contributed to their behaviour—perhaps stress, fear, past trauma, misunderstanding, or simply not knowing a better way to handle the situation. Reflect on times you've acted unskilfully, recognising the common humanity in mistakes and unintended harm. Notice how this understanding shapes your response—maintaining boundaries and consequences while addressing the situation with composure, rather than reacting with anger.

48

Building Healthy Communities

'True community is built on mutual respect and appreciation of differences, not on forced uniformity. The strength of any group comes from the diverse contributions of its members, like different instruments creating a symphony.'

Reflection

The forest thrives
not through rows of identical trees
but through diversity of species,
each offering unique gifts
to the ecosystem.
The body functions
through specialised organs,
none trying to be what they are not.
So, too, human community—
finding harmony not in sameness
but in the complementary dance
of distinct yet interconnected parts.

Meditation

Consider a community you belong to—family, workplace, spiritual group, or neighbourhood. Visualise the different individuals who compose this community, appreciating the unique qualities, perspectives, and contributions each person brings. Reflect on moments when differences within the community created creative tension or conflict. Without judgement, consider how these same differences, when respected, also create resilience and creative potential. Imagine this community as an ecosystem or orchestra where diversity is not merely tolerated but essential to the whole. What might change if differences were more fully honoured and integrated?

Chapter 9

Navigating Change and Impermanence

CHANGE IS THE ONE CONSTANT IN OUR LIVES, YET WE OFTEN struggle against it, seeking permanence in an impermanent world. From minor daily fluctuations to major life transitions and death itself, impermanence defines our existence. Our resistance to this fundamental reality creates much of our suffering while understanding and accepting it brings wisdom and freedom.

The Dalai Lama teaches that contemplating impermanence is not meant to induce anxiety or despair but to awaken us to the preciousness of each moment and help us prioritise what truly matters. When we recognise that everything is in flux—our bodies, thoughts, relationships, possessions—we can hold life more lightly while paradoxically appreciating it more deeply.

This chapter explores how to make peace with impermanence and discover deeper stability amidst life's inevitable changes. We begin by examining how our craving for permanence creates suffering and how accepting the reality of change allows us to appreciate each moment's unique value rather than grasping at what must inevitably transform. The Dalai Lama's teachings on death awareness—a central practice in Tibetan Buddhism—show how contemplating our mortality helps cut through triviality and focus on what gives life genuine meaning.

Here, we learn to view challenges as growth opportunities rather than obstacles to overcome or avoid. Through this transformed relationship with impermanence, we discover a profound peace that doesn't depend on external stability but emerges from within, even in the face of life's greatest uncertainties.

49

The Suffering of Grasping

'Craving for permanence in a world of constant change creates suffering. When we fully accept impermanence, we learn to appreciate each moment's unique value rather than grasp what must inevitably change.'

Reflection

The sunset's beauty lies partly
in its briefness.
The cherry blossom's poignancy
in its swift fading.
The embrace of loved ones
in its unrepeatable uniqueness.
What if all life's moments
were seen this way—
not as possessions to clutch,
but as gifts to witness
in their passing?

Meditation

Begin by focusing on your breath, noticing how each one arises, peaks, and fades without effort. Expand your awareness to bodily sensations, observing their natural fluctuations—tension may arise and dissolve, or warmth may spread and recede. Think of something in your life you're grasping or resisting—perhaps a relationship or a role. Notice the tension this creates. Experiment with loosening your grip; care with open palms rather than clenched fists. Observe how appreciation deepens when you're not trying to hold onto a moment.

50
The Certainty of Death

'Death is certain, but its timing is uncertain. This isn't meant to create anxiety but to help us prioritise what truly matters and not waste our precious human life on trivial concerns.'

Reflection

The hourglass empties
whether watched or ignored.
Not to darken joy with morbidity
but to burnish each moment
with the polish of awareness.
When I acknowledge the horizon,
how much clearer the path becomes,
how much lighter my steps
without unnecessary baggage.

Meditation

Begin by settling your mind with a few minutes of calm breathing. Then reflect, with gentle awareness rather than anxiety: 'Death is certain for all who are born. My death is certain.' Observe any resistance to this contemplation, allowing it to be present without judgement. Continue: 'The time of my death is uncertain. It could come today, tomorrow, or years from now.' Again, observe your response to this truth. Finally, consider: 'What will matter most when I reach the end of my life? What will I value having done, said, or cultivated?' Let these questions illuminate your priorities. As you close, renew your appreciation for this day, this very moment of being alive, with all its possibilities.

51

Remembering Mortality

'Remember that one day you are going to die. We often avoid this truth, but contemplating our mortality helps us prioritise what truly matters in this precious human life.'

Reflection

The clock ticks,
sand falls through the glass,
petals drop from the flower.
Not to instil fear,
but to awaken appreciation
for this breath,
this moment,
this unrepeatable day.
Death is life's most patient teacher
of what truly matters.

Meditation

Sit quietly and imagine that you have only one year left to live. (If this creates too much anxiety, you can extend the timeframe to five years.) With this perspective, reflect: What becomes important? What falls away as insignificant? How would you spend your time differently? What relationships would you prioritise or heal? What would you want to express or create? What inner qualities would you want to develop? Observe how this contemplation clarifies your values and priorities in the present moment. Conclude by feeling gratitude for the time you do have, however long or short it may be.

52

What Matters at Life's End

'When facing death, what brings peace is not the quantity of what we've accumulated but the quality of how we've lived—especially the warmth and compassion we've shown to others.'

Reflection

The final accounting
asks not what we owned
but what we gave,
not what we achieved
but how we loved,
not the impressions we made
but the kindness we embodied.
The wealth that matters
cannot be inherited,
except as inspiration
for those who witness
a life well-lived.

Meditation

Reflect on your inevitable death. Imagine you are at the end of your life, looking back over the journey. From this perspective, explore: What actions and qualities bring you a sense of fulfilment and peace? Are they aligned with how you're currently investing your time and energy? What do you wish you had given more attention to? What do you regret having prioritised? What would you want others to remember about how you lived and who you were? Let these reflections guide how you prioritise your time and energy today, recognising that you are creating the life you will one day revisit.

53
The Natural Flow of Existence

'Experiencing the process of ageing, illness, and the approach of death as part of the natural flow of existence brings a profound peace. Our resistance to these inevitable processes creates much of our suffering.'

Reflection

The autumn leaf doesn't rage
against its changing colour.
The wave doesn't protest
its return to the ocean.
The day doesn't resist
its transition to night.
What freedom might arise
if we could see our own unfolding
with the same accepting clarity,
recognising each stage
as neither punishment nor mistake
but nature expressing itself through us?

Meditation

Observe the natural cycles visible in the world around you—day and night, seasons, growth and decay, the constant change that characterises all life. Reflect on how your own body and mind participate in these same cycles. Consider how ageing, illness, and eventually death are not personal affronts but participation in the broader rhythm of existence that all living things share. If resistance arises to these thoughts, acknowledge it kindly. Explore the fears or beliefs behind it. Embrace your life process with the same acceptance as autumn leaves changing colour or day turning to night—natural and beautiful in its own way.

54
Transforming Adversity

'We cannot eliminate adversity,
but we can change how we respond to it.
By viewing challenges as opportunities for growth
and understanding, we transform what would be
suffering into a path of development.'

Reflection

The fire that threatens to consume
becomes, with proper tending,
the heat that forges strength.
The weight that might crush
becomes, with proper stance,
the resistance that builds muscle.
The crisis that seems only loss
reveals, with proper attention,
doorways to depths
we would never otherwise explore.

Meditation

Identify a current difficulty in your life. Bring it to mind with as much clarity as possible, acknowledging its reality and impact without minimising or exaggerating. Observe your habitual response to this challenge. Is there resistance, avoidance, or a sense of being victimised? Note these reactions without judgement. Then shift perspective, asking yourself: What quality might this difficulty help me develop? What understanding might it reveal that I couldn't access otherwise? How might this challenge serve as a teacher or catalyst for necessary growth? While maintaining realistic acknowledgement of the difficulty, experiment with relating to it as potential transformation rather than mere obstacle. Observe how this perspective shift changes your relationship to the situation.

Chapter 10

Finding Purpose and Meaning

WHAT GIVES LIFE ITS MOST PROFOUND SIGNIFICANCE? Beyond material success or fleeting pleasures, the Dalai Lama points to the deep fulfilment that comes from aligning our lives with meaningful values and purpose. In a world often focused on external achievements and acquisition, his teachings invite us to look deeper—to the qualities of mind and heart that create lasting well-being for ourselves and others.

The search for meaning is universal, transcending cultural and religious boundaries. Whether expressed through spiritual traditions, philosophical inquiry, or simply the quiet questioning of our own hearts, we all seek to understand what makes life worthwhile. The Dalai Lama's approach to this perennial question is both profound and practical, grounded in the reality of our shared human condition rather than abstract ideals.

This chapter explores the Buddhist view of purpose and meaning, beginning with the fundamental insight that the purpose of life is happiness rooted in compassionate heart and clear mind. We examine the crucial distinction between pleasure and genuine happiness, discovering that what we often pursue in the name of happiness may actually undermine it.

Through these teachings, we learn that purpose isn't something we need to invent or impose, but rather something we uncover by aligning with the deepest truths of our interdependent existence. When we diminish self-centredness and expand our circle of concern, we find meaning not as an abstract concept but as the lived experience of connection and contribution.

55
The Purpose of Life

'The purpose of our lives is to be happy. It is not shallow, pleasure-based happiness, but deep satisfaction that comes from a compassionate heart and a clear mind. Each of us has the capacity and responsibility to create such meaningful happiness, not just for ourselves but for our world.'

Reflection

The search that led us
through countless doors,
across mountains of philosophy,
through the valleys of practice,
arrives at this simple truth:
We were born for joy—
not the fleeting delight of acquisition,
but the enduring contentment
of a life well-lived,
a heart fully opened,
a mind deeply awakened.
This is our birthright and our gift to all beings.

Meditation

Sit quietly and reflect on what brings you genuine, lasting happiness rather than temporary pleasure. Consider the moments when you've felt most fulfilled and at peace. Observe what qualities were present—perhaps connection, meaning, generosity, clarity, or compassion. Then reflect on the relationship between your happiness and others' well-being. When has contributing to others' happiness enhanced your own? When has pursuing your happiness at others' expense ultimately left you feeling empty? Set an intention to cultivate these sources of authentic happiness, recognising that your well-being and others are deeply interconnected.

56
Pleasure Versus Happiness

'There is an important distinction between pleasure and happiness. Pleasure is based primarily on physical sensations and is fleeting by nature. Genuine happiness is rooted in the mind—in inner peace, understanding, and compassion. True and lasting happiness comes from mental development and concern for others' welfare.'

Reflection

The feast that leaves us hungry still,
the drink that deepens thirst,
the prize that loses lustre once possessed.
These pleasures rise and fall like waves on water.
Yet beneath the surface currents
lies an ocean of contentment
not dependent on gaining or keeping anything at all—
a wellspring of joy that flows from within.

Meditation

Recall a recent experience of pleasure—perhaps a delicious meal, an entertaining show, or a material purchase. Observe its qualities: How quickly did it arise and fade? Did it leave you satisfied or wanting more? How dependent was it on specific external conditions? Then recall an experience of deeper happiness—perhaps a moment of meaningful connection, an act of generosity, or a period of mental clarity and peace. Observe its different qualities: How did it arise? How long did its effects last? Was it dependent on external circumstances in the same way? Reflect on how society often confuses these two experiences, leading us to pursue pleasure with the hope of finding happiness. Consider how you might orient your life more towards the sources of genuine happiness rather than temporary pleasure.

57

The Warmth of Human Connection

'The basic source of all happiness is a sense of kindness and warm-heartedness towards others. We are all the same as human beings; we all want happiness and not suffering. The moment you begin thinking about the welfare of others, your mind broadens, and your own problems seem smaller.'

Reflection

The closed fist cannot receive.
The hardened heart cannot be filled.
Only in the gesture of opening
do we discover what we truly seek.
Not an emotion to be manufactured
but a quality to be uncovered,
warm-heartedness waits within
like embers beneath the ash.

Meditation

Bring awareness to your heart centre—place a hand there. Recall a time when you naturally felt kind and caring towards others, when concern for their well-being arose spontaneously. Remember how this felt in your body and mind. Now, bring to mind someone you care about who is facing a difficulty. Let yourself feel genuine care for their well-being, wishing for their suffering to ease, and for them to find happiness. Gradually, expand this circle of warm-heartedness to include others—even those you find difficult. You don't need to force intense feelings, just the simple recognition: 'Just like me, this person wishes to be happy and free from suffering.' Observe how this expansion of concern affects your mental state, particularly your perspective on your personal problems.

58
Inner Development as the Source of Happiness

'True happiness comes not from seeking pleasant experiences but from mental development—cultivating qualities like kindness, clarity, and wisdom that remain stable regardless of external circumstances.'

Reflection

Building a house on sand
means living at the mercy of tides.
Chasing pleasant moments
is grasping at reflections in water.
But the qualities cultivated within—
these become the bedrock
that no storm can wash away,
the wealth no thief can steal,
the light no darkness can extinguish.

Meditation

Recall a time when external conditions were challenging, but an inner quality—like patience, courage, or compassion—helped you maintain stability and well-being. Observe how this internal resource supported you when external sources of happiness were unavailable. Then recall a time when external conditions were pleasant, but inner turmoil prevented you from enjoying them. Observe how inner states can override even favourable circumstances. Reflect on which sources of happiness—external or internal—prove more reliable over time. Consider which inner qualities you would like to strengthen as sources of stable well-being, regardless of changing circumstances.

59
Interdependent Well-Being

'If we neglect the welfare of others while pursuing our happiness, ultimately, we will fail in both aims. Our well-being is deeply connected to that of others. This is not idealism—it is a practical reality in our interconnected world.'

Reflection

No island stands
truly apart from the sea.
No joy blooms fully
in the garden of one heart alone.
The cup of my joy, when filled
by taking from yours,
develops invisible cracks.
What seems like gain
becomes subtle loss.
Only when both vessels rise
does the water remain.

Meditation

Recall a time when your happiness depended on someone else's well-being—perhaps when you could only be truly happy if a loved one was also doing well or when your enjoyment of something was enhanced by sharing it. Then, recall a time when focusing solely on your needs ultimately left you feeling disconnected or unfulfilled, even if you got what you wanted. Reflect on experiences where contributing to others' happiness actually increased your own—creating a positive cycle rather than a zero-sum game. Consider how this understanding might reshape your approach to seeking happiness.

60
Beyond Self-Centredness

'The essence of spiritual practice is to diminish self-centredness and expand our circle of concern. As we do this, we discover that our own happiness is intimately connected to the well-being of others.'

Reflection

The tight fist of 'me and mine'
slowly unfurling
to reveal an open palm.
The narrow spotlight of self-concern
gradually widening
to illuminate a larger stage.
The boundary between self and other
not violently erased
but gently blurred
through recognition of our common ground,
our shared vulnerability and hopes.

Meditation

Expand your circle of concern by acknowledging your natural concern for your own well-being. There's nothing wrong with wishing for your happiness—it's a starting point, not something to transcend completely. Then, bring to mind someone you love deeply. Allow your concern for others' well-being to arise naturally, noting how it feels in your heart. Is it separate from your own care, or a natural extension? Gradually expand this circle to include acquaintances and strangers, repeating: 'Just as I wish to be happy and free from suffering, may they be happy and free from suffering.' Observe how this practice affects your sense of connection and well-being—does it feel constraining or expanding?

Chapter 11

Ethical Living in Today's World

How do we live with integrity in a complex, rapidly changing world? This question becomes increasingly challenging as we navigate ethical dilemmas that previous generations never faced—from environmental sustainability to digital ethics, from global inequalities to the accelerating pace of technological change.

The Dalai Lama teaches that genuine ethics emerges not from rigid rules but from understanding the consequences of our actions and developing genuine concern for others' well-being. Rather than imposing external commandments, Buddhism encourages developing ethical awareness by recognising how our actions affect ourselves and others across time. When we see clearly the causal connections between choices and their effects, ethical conduct becomes not a constraint but a natural expression of wisdom and compassion.

This chapter explores how to bring ethical awareness to our relationships, work, consumption choices, and social engagement. We examine how ethics arises from understanding consequences rather than merely following rules, and how our actions shape not only our external world but also our consciousness and character. The Dalai Lama's teachings on secular ethics emphasise that anyone, regardless of religious affiliation, can practice core values like compassion, forgiveness, and self-discipline.

We discover that ethical living is not a restriction but a path to greater freedom and harmony with ourselves and our world. When our actions align with our deepest values, we experience the integrity and peace that comes from wholeness—from being undivided against ourselves and in genuine relationship with the wider community of life.

61

Ethics Beyond Rules

'Ethics isn't about conforming to external rules but about recognising how our actions affect ourselves and others. When we see clearly the consequences of harmful actions, ethical conduct becomes natural.'

Reflection

The child learns not to touch fire
not from obedience to rules
but from experiencing the burn.
So too the mature heart
avoids harm not from fear
of punishment or judgement,
but from intimate knowledge
of how suffering spreads
through the web of connection.

Meditation

Recall a time when you acted in a way that caused harm to yourself or others. Without judgement, carefully trace the consequences of that action—how it affected your mind, your relationships, and your subsequent choices. Then recall a time when you acted with integrity, even when it was difficult. Again, trace the effects of that action on yourself and others. Observe how this clarity about consequences naturally inclines the mind towards ethical action, without the need for rigid rules imposed from outside. Reflect on an area of your life where greater ethical awareness could lead to more skilful choices. What specific consequences might you need to become more aware of?

62

Character Shaped by Choices

'Our ethical choices shape our consciousness.
Every time we act with integrity and compassion,
we strengthen those qualities within us;
every time we act from greed or hatred,
we reinforce those tendencies.'

Reflection

Each choice, a chisel stroke
on the statue of becoming.
Each action, a brushstroke
on the canvas of character.
Nothing lost, nothing wasted—
all gathered into the reservoir
of habit and inclination
from which tomorrow's thoughts
and impulses will arise.
We create ourselves
choice by choice, day by day.

Meditation

Reflect on the relationship between your actions and your character. Consider a quality you wish to develop more fully in yourself (such as patience, generosity, or courage). Recall instances when you've acted in accordance with this quality, even in small ways. Observe how each action made it slightly easier to act this way again, creating a positive pattern. Then, consider a quality you'd like to diminish (such as reactivity, selfishness, or fearfulness). Recall how acting from this quality strengthens its hold on you. Reflect on the profound truth that you become what you repeatedly do—your actions shape your character, which then influences your future actions in an ongoing cycle. Consider how this understanding gives new significance to even small daily choices.

63

Compassionate Flexibility

'Our ethical actions should be guided by their effects on others, not by rigid rules. Sometimes compassion requires breaking convention if it genuinely serves others' welfare.'

Reflection

The map is not the territory;
the recipe is not the meal.
Rules carved in stone
lack the wisdom to bend
when compassion demands flexibility.
Better the living compass
of a heart trained to recognise
suffering and respond with skill,
than blind adherence
to yesterday's certainties.

Meditation

Recall a situation where following a rule or convention would have caused harm or where breaking one prevented harm. Reflect on how discernment and compassionate intention factor into ethical decisions more than rigid adherence to rules. What guided your decision in that moment? Consider an area of your life where you might be applying ethical principles too rigidly or too loosely. What would a more balanced approach look like—one that honours both universal principles and the unique demands of specific situations? Contemplate how to develop both strong ethical principles and the wisdom to apply them flexibly according to circumstances.

64

Ethics for Everyone

'Ethics are not the property of any religion. The core ethical values—compassion, forgiveness, self-discipline, generosity, contentment—can be practised by anyone, whether religious or not. In fact, I believe we can develop a secular approach to ethics based on our shared humanity and common desire for happiness.'

Reflection

Beyond the temples and the texts,
beyond the rituals and robes,
lies the essence of all wisdom:
to live with kindness towards all beings.
No special language needed,
no initiation required—
only the recognition that your happiness and mine
grow from the same soil of care.

Meditation

Identify one ethical value (such as compassion, honesty, or respect) that resonates with you deeply. Reflect on how this value is recognised across different cultural and religious traditions, albeit expressed in different ways. Consider how this value is grounded in our shared human condition—how it arises from our nature as social beings who depend on one another and share common needs and vulnerabilities. Contemplate how you might practise this value in your daily life, independent of any particular religious framework.

65
Ethical Consumption

'Our excessive consumption is not just an environmental issue but a spiritual one. It reflects an inner emptiness we try to fill with possessions when we truly need meaning, connection, and the contentment that comes from knowing what is enough.'

Reflection

The closets overflow
with unworn clothes,
the shelves sag
with unread books,
the storage units multiply
with forgotten treasures—
all testament to the hungry ghost
that feeds but never fills,
consumes but never satisfies,
accumulates but never feels
the wealth of 'enough.'

Meditation

Reflect on a recent non-essential purchase. What need were you trying to meet? Was it a physical necessity or an emotional hunger? Did the purchase satisfy that need in a lasting way? Consider how consumption affects not just your material circumstances but your state of mind. When does acquiring more create satisfaction, and when does it create more wanting? Contemplate the wider impacts of your consumption patterns—on the environment, workers who produce what you buy, financial well-being, and inner state of contentment or dissatisfaction. Explore what 'enough' might mean for you in different areas of life. What is the difference between genuine need and conditioned want?

66
Compassionate Systems

'Political and economic systems matter greatly, but without compassion at their foundation, even the best systems can become corrupt. Compassion must be the motivation behind our social structures, not just an afterthought.'

Reflection

Laws without heart become oppressive.
Markets without care become exploitation.
Power without compassion becomes tyranny.
The most brilliant architecture
built on a foundation of sand
cannot long endure.
So too, our human systems
without the bedrock of genuine concern
for the welfare of all.

Meditation

Consider a social or political issue that matters to you. Rather than viewing it solely through the lens of your beliefs or preferred solutions, reflect on how compassion might shape how we approach this issue—regardless of our political stance. Imagine what policies and public discourse might look like if genuine concern for all those affected were the starting point.Reflect on how your personal ethical values connect to broader social questions. How might your daily choices contribute to more compassionate systems? Consider how individual transformation and system change are interconnected—neither sufficient alone, but powerful when aligned.

Chapter 12

Joy and Contentment

JOY IS NOT MERELY AN EMOTION, BUT A QUALITY OF BEING that can be cultivated through consistent practice. The Dalai Lama, known for his warmth and joyful laughter, teaches that genuine joy arises from inner contentment rather than external circumstances. This perspective challenges our culture's tendency to pursue happiness by acquiring more—more possessions, more experiences, more accomplishments—and instead points us towards the richness of our present experience.

This chapter explores practices that nurture joy, appreciation, and a sense of sufficiency—qualities that remain accessible even amid life's inevitable challenges. We begin by examining the 'eight worldly concerns' that keep us trapped in cycles of hope and fear, comparing ourselves to others and endlessly chasing satisfaction that proves elusive. By recognising how these concerns operate in our lives, we can gradually free ourselves from their grip and discover a more stable sense of contentment.

The Dalai Lama teaches that happiness relies more on our mental attitude than on external conditions. A restless mind will suffer even with material comfort, while a well-trained mind can find joy in difficult circumstances. This perspective emphasises that happiness is cultivated internally rather than pursued externally.

Through these teachings, we discover that joy is not just a pleasant state but a profound spiritual resource that sustains us on the path. When we free ourselves from constant craving for different circumstances and appreciate what we have, we tap into a wellspring of contentment that remains available regardless of external conditions.

67
Beyond the Eight Worldly Concerns

'The eight worldly concerns—hope for gain and fear of loss, pleasure and fear of pain, praise and blame, hope for fame and insignificance—keep us churning in discontent. True peace comes from transcending these concerns.'

Reflection

Gaining and losing,
praised and blamed,
famous and forgotten,
pleased and pained—
this endless teeter-totter
keeps the heart restless,
the mind anxious,
the spirit fragmented.
What freedom might come
from stepping off this wheel,
finding ground that doesn't shift
with every changing wind?

Meditation

Reflect on each pair of concerns, noticing how they create ongoing tension in your experience: Hope for gain and fear of loss, craving for pleasure and aversion to pain, desire for praise and fear of criticism, and wish for fame/recognition and fear of insignificance. Identify which of these pairs has the strongest hold on you. When does it most strongly influence your choices and emotional states? Imagine what it would feel like to be less driven by these concerns—not indifferent to life's natural pleasures and pains but less defined and controlled by them. Consider what values or aspirations might provide a more stable foundation for your well-being than these fluctuating worldly concerns.

68

The Mind as Source of Happiness

'Happiness relates more to our state of mind than our circumstances. Even in comfortable conditions, a restless, discontented mind will find suffering. Yet even in difficulty, a peaceful mind can find joy.'

Reflection

The prisoner in the palace,
restless with wanting more.
The sage in the simple hut,
content with precisely this.
Surrounded by luxury,
yet starving for satisfaction.
Having little by the world's measure,
yet lacking nothing essential.
The mind creates its own landscape,
far more real than external scenery.

Meditation

Recall a time when you had favourable external conditions but still felt dissatisfied or unhappy. What mental states or attitudes prevented you from enjoying the good circumstances? Then, recall when you faced challenging external conditions but maintained a sense of inner peace or joy. What mental qualities allowed you to remain stable despite the difficulties? Reflect on the profound truth that while we often can't control external circumstances, we can develop greater mastery over our inner responses to them. Consider which mental qualities you'd like to strengthen to nurture greater happiness independent of circumstances—perhaps gratitude, acceptance, generosity, or equanimity.

69
Rejoicing in Others' Good Fortune

'Rejoicing in others' good qualities and success is a powerful practice that turns the poison of envy into the medicine of inspiration and shared joy.'

Reflection

When I see your light,
I can diminish it with a comparison
or magnify it with appreciation.
One path leads to scarcity—
a world where your gain
must mean my loss.
The other reveals abundance—
your joy becomes mine,
your gifts enrich us all,
and the heart expands
beyond its jealous borders.

Meditation

Begin by considering someone whose success, happiness, or good qualities you can readily appreciate. Experience genuine delight in their good fortune, as if celebrating a dear friend's birthday. Then, bring to mind someone towards whom you might typically feel competitive or envious. With gentle effort, appreciate something positive about them. Observe the difference between envy (contracted, bitter) and appreciative joy (expansive, connected). Reflect on how rejoicing in others' good fortune actually increases your own happiness.

70
Appreciating What Is

'Appreciating our current situation—including our difficulties—helps us avoid creating unnecessary suffering through constant comparison with an imagined 'better' state. This doesn't mean passive acceptance but clearly seeing what is.'

Reflection

The mind, ever restless,
leans forward into dreams
or drifts backward through shadows.
But the ground beneath our feet
is not a stepping stone to elsewhere—
it is the path itself.
Even the cracked places
glint with morning dew
if seen in the right light.
To pause, to truly see,
is to find hidden grace
in the fabric of what already is.

Meditation

Sit quietly and consider an aspect of your life that feels incomplete or difficult. Without trying to fix or change it, observe it closely. Name what is present—emotion, sensation, thought. Ask gently: 'What is here that I haven't yet appreciated?' Look for hidden lessons, strengths, or beauty, even within discomfort. Let this be a meditation not on perfection but on presence.

71

Inner Peace as Foundation for Action

'Inner peace is not passive withdrawal but the foundation for effective action. Like a martial artist who must be centred before executing a powerful move, our social engagement becomes more effective when it comes from a place of inner calm.'

Reflection

The eye of the hurricane
is not disengaged from the storm
but it's still a generative centre.
The roots of the oak
do not represent an escape from the world
but the source of strength
that allows its branches to reach skyward.
So, too, our inner cultivation—
not retreat from life's demands
but a preparation to meet them
with power and precision.

Meditation

Begin with mindful breathing to establish a stable inner state. Consider a current challenge and observe how it feels from this calm place. Consider how reactivity differs from a grounded response. Reflect on what helps you remain centred while actively engaging with life's demands.

72
The Power of Optimism

'I find hope in the darkest days and focus in the brightest. Choose to be optimistic—it feels better! This is not naivety but a recognition that our mental attitude is something we can train.
A joyful mind is powerful and can benefit others and face challenges without losing heart.'

Reflection

The rain falls equally
on blossoming gardens and barren ground.
What differs is not the water
but the soil that receives it.
So, too, with life's events—
joy comes not from perfect circumstances
but from how we engage with what comes.
The trained mind finds gold in gravel,
possibility in the very air we breathe.

Meditation

Nurture realistic optimism by bringing to mind a difficulty you face. Acknowledge its reality. Then widen your perspective: What strengths do you bring to it? What lessons might emerge? What small opportunities exist within it? How might someone wise approach it? Reflect on how this broader view influences your emotional state and response.

Chapter 13

Meditation Practice

MEDITATION LIES AT THE HEART OF BUDDHIST PRACTICE and the Dalai Lama's teachings. Far from merely a relaxation technique, meditation is a systematic mind training that develops clarity, stability, and insight. Through consistent practice, we cultivate qualities that transform our experience and world.

The Dalai Lama often emphasises that meditation is not about escaping reality but seeing it more clearly. In the Buddhist tradition, meditation encompasses many practices—from developing single-pointed concentration to generating compassion, from analytical investigation to resting in open awareness. Different practices serve different purposes, creating a comprehensive approach to mental training.

This chapter explores practical aspects of meditation—how to establish a consistent practice, overcome common obstacles, and integrate meditative awareness into daily life. The Dalai Lama teaches that even brief, regular practice is more beneficial than occasional long sessions. He encourages a balanced approach that incorporates both formal sitting practice and the application of awareness throughout our daily activities.

73
Building a Regular Practice

'A few moments of genuine meditation practice each day is more valuable than meditating for hours only occasionally. Like watering a plant, a little each day rather than drenching it once a month, consistency matters more than duration.'

Reflection

The mighty river that carves canyons
begins as a steady trickle.
The towering tree that withstands storms
grows through daily increments too small to see.
So, too, with meditation—
not heroic bursts of effort,
but the gentle persistence
of showing up day after day,
moment by moment,
that transforms the landscape of the mind.

Meditation

Begin by acknowledging your intention to develop a regular meditation practice. Recognise that this intention is valuable regardless of how consistently you've practised in the past. Reflect on the conditions that support your practice—perhaps a specific time of day, a dedicated space, certain reminders, or accountability to others. Consider the obstacles that arise—busyness, forgetting, discomfort, or discouragement. Explore how you might work with each one kindly rather than harshly. Set realistic intentions for the coming week. Be specific about when and for how long you'll meditate, choosing consistency over ambitious but unsustainable goals.

74
Working with Obstacles

'In meditation, obstacles like restlessness, drowsiness, or discouragement are not failures but opportunities to develop important skills. Learning to work with these challenges is itself a crucial part of the practice.'

Reflection

The skilled sailor doesn't curse the wind
but learns to read its patterns,
adjusting sails to harness
even contrary forces.
The waves that threatened to capsize
become, with practice,
the very energy that propels the journey.
So, too, with meditation's challenges—
not enemies to vanquish
but teachers in disguise.

Meditation

Begin with a few minutes of stable attention on the breath. As obstacles arise (and they will), respond based on their nature. For restlessness or agitation, recognise its energy and shift attention to bodily sensations. Ground yourself in the feeling of weight or contact with the floor. For drowsiness or dullness, refresh your attention—straighten your posture, open your eyes slightly, or focus on sharper sensations like the beginning of each breath. When caught in thought, neither suppress nor follow them. Label gently ('planning', 'remembering', or 'judging') and return to the breath. Notice how these challenges cultivate discernment, resilience, and flexibility.

75

Integrating Meditation into Daily Life

'The true measure of meditation is not what happens on the cushion but how it transforms your daily life. Every activity can become an opportunity for practising awareness, patience, and compassion.'

Reflection

The boundary blurs
between formal practice and daily living,
between sacred and ordinary moments.
The cushion becomes a training ground
for life's messy, beautiful complexity;
life becomes the proving ground
for cushion-cultivated qualities.
Until eventually we see:
There was never a separation—
only one continuous opportunity
to be fully present.

Meditation

Begin with five minutes of focused meditation on the breath, cultivating clear, stable awareness. Then broaden your attention for another five minutes to include sounds, bodily sensations, and thoughts—maintaining the same calm clarity. Finally, spend five minutes imagining how you might carry this presence into a real-life activity today—perhaps a meeting, a routine task, or a conversation. Reflect on how your meditation skills can directly support your actions, responses, and daily choices.

76

Finding the Right Balance

'Different meditation techniques serve different purposes. Concentration builds stability, analytical meditation develops insight, and heart practices cultivate positive qualities.
A balanced practice incorporates all these elements according to your needs.'

Reflection

The inner field does not bloom
through effort alone,
but through wise tending.
Stillness anchors the roots.
Inquiry turns the soil.
Loving presence warms each sprout.
Each method, like a seasoned tool,
serves its season and need—
no blade where water is required,
no fire where shade will do.
To meditate well
is not to master one path,
but to walk among many,
knowing when to pause,
when to dig deeper,
and when to simply be.

Meditation

Experience three types of meditation: (1) Stabilisation (6–7 minutes)—focus on the breath at the nostrils, gently returning when the mind wanders to build clarity. (2) Analytical (6–7 minutes)—reflect on questions like 'What is the mind?' and use this focus to investigate. (3) Heart-based (6–7 minutes)—cultivate loving-kindness, starting with yourself and extending to others. Notice how each technique nurtures different qualities and fosters a balanced inner life.

77

The Role of the Body

'In meditation, the body is not something to transcend but a foundation for practice. Proper posture, breath awareness, and physical presence create mental clarity and stability conditions.'

Reflection

The temple and its offerings are one.
The instrument and its music, inseparable.
This body—not a cage to escape,
but the very ground of awakening,
the sacred vessel through which
awareness flows and flourishes.
Each sensation a gateway,
each breath a bridge
between material and immaterial realms,
uniting what was never truly divided.

Meditation

Return to the body as anchor and ally. Sit upright, comfortably balanced between effort and ease. Take a few moments to adjust until the posture feels both alert and relaxed. Bring attention to physical contact points—feet on the ground, back against the chair, air on your skin. Let your awareness settle here. Shift to the breath, not only at the nostrils but as a whole-body experience. Feel the movement in the torso, the expansion and release. If the mind wanders, gently return to these sensations. Let the body draw you back to now, again and again, with patience.

78

Finding Joy in Practice

'Meditation should not be approached as a grim duty but with an attitude of joyful exploration. When we discover the natural delight in being fully present, practice becomes self-sustaining rather than effortful.'

Reflection

The child does not study wonder—
it rises unbidden
when space and silence allow.
The musician does not force music—
she listens, surrenders,
lets the melody carry her home.
So, too, with meditation.
Beyond posture and method,
beyond effort and form,
there waits a quiet joy—
not something achieved,
but something remembered.
The sheer relief
of no longer reaching,
of resting in the soft brilliance
of this breath,
this moment,
this being.

Meditation

Approach practice as joyful engagement, letting go of obligation and performance. Enter with openness, like exploring a new trail. Be curious about the texture of your breath and the emotions surfacing. Notice small pleasures—ease in an exhale, relief in letting go, and peace in simply being. If boredom or frustration arises, meet them with curiosity, as every state has something to teach.

Chapter 14

Science and Buddhism

THE RELATIONSHIP BETWEEN SCIENCE AND SPIRITUALITY IS often portrayed as conflict or mutual exclusion. Yet the Dalai Lama has been engaged in ongoing dialogue with scientists for decades, finding remarkable convergence between Buddhist insights and scientific discoveries about the mind and reality. Far from seeing science as a threat to spiritual understanding, he celebrates how these different approaches to knowledge can complement and enrich each other.

In the Buddhist approach, empirical investigation has always been valued alongside contemplative inquiry. The Buddha himself encouraged his followers not to accept teachings on authority alone but to test them through personal experience. This emphasis on investigation rather than blind faith creates natural common ground with the scientific method, even as the two traditions employ different tools and address various questions.

This chapter explores the intersection of Buddhism and science, focusing on neuroscience research on meditation and physics discoveries that align with Buddhist concepts of interdependence and emptiness. It highlights how neuroplasticity supports the Buddhist idea that the mind can be trained to cultivate positive traits and reduce negative tendencies.

The Dalai Lama teaches that science and Buddhism are committed to truth, even when findings challenge existing beliefs. This open, evolving quality allows both traditions to grow through dialogue. Science enhances our understanding of the physical world, while Buddhism provides insights into subjective experience and ethical wisdom. Together, they offer complementary views on human existence.

79
Convergent Paths to Knowledge

'My ongoing conversations with scientists have been tremendously beneficial. Where science and spirituality meet, both are enhanced. Science offers precision in understanding the material world, while Buddhist practice addresses the inner transformation needed for genuine happiness.'

Reflection

The microscope and the meditation cushion:
two tools of investigation,
two paths of discovery.
One peers into the quantum dance,
the other into the nature of mind itself.
When these rivers of inquiry converge,
how much richer the understanding
of this mysterious existence we share.

Meditation

Reflect on a scientific insight that has broadened your understanding of the world, such as evolution or the cosmos, and how this enriches your perspective. Consider a personal moment of insight—like clarity about your thoughts or a feeling of interconnection—and value this first-person experience. Acknowledge how objective and subjective investigations complement each other, as neither offers a complete picture. Contemplate how scientific understanding can inform your spiritual practice and how personal insights can enrich your scientific knowledge.

80
Neuroplasticity and Mind Training

'I have been meeting with neuroscientists for many years now, and they have shown through research what Buddhist practitioners have long understood—that the brain is remarkably plastic, capable of transformation through sustained mental training.'

Reflection

What once seemed fixed as stone—
the grooves of habit,
the channels of reaction,
the entrenched patterns of thought—
science now confirms
can flow like water,
finding new paths,
carving fresh possibilities.
The mind rewrites itself
through its own attention,
the contemplative and the scientist
arriving at the same hopeful truth.

Meditation

Reflect on a habit you once thought was fixed but changed through practice—perhaps your response to stress or your attitude towards yourself or others. This illustrates neuroplasticity, the brain's ability to rewire itself. Identify a current pattern you want to transform. Recognise that change is possible with consistent effort, and set an intention to work on this pattern through both structured practice and everyday awareness. This understanding of the mind's malleability provides a balanced view between determinism ('I'm just made this way') and unrealistic expectations of instant change.

81
Physics and Buddhist Philosophy

'Modern physics describes a reality of extraordinary interconnectedness, where observer and observed cannot be separated. This scientific understanding aligns remarkably with Buddhist insights about emptiness and interdependence developed thousands of years ago.'

Reflection

The physicist and the meditator
arrive at the same revelation
through different instruments:
There is no solid world
apart from perception,
no independent observer
separate from the observed.
Subject and object
arise together,
two faces of one process,
like wave and water,
inseparable.

Meditation

Bring awareness to a perception, like seeing an object or hearing a sound. Notice that this experience encompasses both the perceived and the act of perceiving, which depend on each other. Reflect on how this parallels insights from quantum physics (the observer affects the observed) and Buddhist philosophy (reality as interdependent). Contemplate how your presence and attention are integral to a dynamic process, shifting your relationship with the world from an isolated observer to a participant in an interconnected experience.

82
Research on Meditation

'Scientific studies of experienced meditators show measurable changes in brain function and structure. This research validates what practitioners have known—that systematic mental training creates lasting positive changes in attention, emotion regulation, and well-being.'

Reflection

What sages once touched
in the stillness of mountain caves,
science now glimpses
in pulses of light and magnetic resonance.
Not to diminish the sacred,
but to decode its echo—
to listen again,
this time through instruments and graphs.
The brain scans flicker
where the breath slows,
and the ancient silence speaks
in a new tongue.
When the inner cosmos
meets the microscope's gaze,
we do not choose between
mystery and measurement—
we learn to bow to both.

Meditation

Begin with an attention exercise, focusing on your breath for 5–7 minutes. Notice how your attention wanders and returns. Reflect on how sustained attention activates specific brain regions and strengthens networks involved in focus over time. Then practise a compassion meditation, wishing well for others. Observe your experience and research findings on how such practices affect empathy, positive emotions, stress hormones, and social behaviour. Appreciate how both personal experience and scientific insights enhance understanding of these practices.

83
The Science of Compassion

'Research now demonstrates what compassion practitioners have long experienced—that training in compassion reduces stress hormones, strengthens immune function, and activates brain regions associated with positive emotion and connection. Science and contemplative wisdom converge in affirming compassion's benefits.'

Reflection

What was once called softness,
dismissed as sentiment or soul's indulgence,
now stands affirmed—
not in poetry alone,
but in the language of data and pulse.
Compassion, it turns out,
is not just noble,
but necessary.
It lowers blood pressure,
calms inflammation,
softens fear.
The heart, when open,
becomes its own kind of physician—
radiating a warmth
that heals both giver and receiver.
Ancient truths,
now seen through the microscope,
whisper again what we've always known:
To care is to cure.

Meditation

Begin by cultivating compassion for yourself. Place a hand on your heart and wish for your well-being: 'May I be free from suffering. May I find peace.' Gradually extend these wishes to loved ones, neutral individuals, those you find difficult, and all beings. Visualise sending care with each breath. Research shows this practice can reduce inflammation, lower stress hormones, activate positive emotion areas in the brain, and strengthen immune function. Reflect on how these benefits might enhance your motivation and engagement.

84
The Limitations of Both Approaches

'Science and Buddhism both have their limitations and strengths. Science excels at understanding the physical world but has less to say about meaning, ethics, and consciousness itself. Buddhism offers sophisticated methods for investigating subjective experience, but benefits from science's precision in studying material causes.'

Reflection

One lens scans the stars—
charting vast galaxies,
naming distant light.
The other turns inward,
tracing the silence
from which all thought arises.
One speaks in data,
the other in stillness.
Yet neither alone
can name the whole.
The microscope may unveil the cell,
but not the ache of longing.
Meditation may glimpse awareness itself,
but not the atom's dance.
These are not rival truths,
but twin flames—
each illuminating
what the other cannot reach.
Together, they make the invisible visible,
and the unspeakable known.

Meditation

Consider a significant question in your life—about consciousness, ethics, or the meaning of life. How might scientific understanding inform this? What can be observed and measured, and what insights has science provided? Next, reflect on the contributions of contemplative wisdom. Which aspects involve subjective experience or values that resist material explanations? Think about how combining these perspectives can deepen understanding. How might science enhance contemplative insights, and how could wisdom shape the application of scientific knowledge?

Chapter 15

Interfaith Harmony

In a world where religious differences often fuel conflict, the Dalai Lama offers a powerful vision of interfaith harmony based on mutual respect and appreciation. Having engaged with leaders and practitioners from diverse traditions throughout his life, he emphasises that all major religions share core ethical teachings—the importance of love, compassion, forgiveness, and tolerance—even as they differ in philosophical approaches and practices.

This perspective doesn't require diluting distinct traditions into a homogeneous blend. Instead, it recognises the value of diversity while finding common ground in shared human values. The Dalai Lama often points out that different religions serve different temperaments and cultural contexts—like various medicines treating the same illness through different approaches, each valuable for particular people.

This chapter explores the foundations of genuine interfaith dialogue—not as a means to convert others but as an opportunity for mutual enrichment and greater understanding. We examine how respecting differences while celebrating commonalities creates the basis for harmony that transcends mere tolerance. The Dalai Lama teaches that when religious leaders meet in mutual respect, it sends a powerful message that spiritual values transcend doctrinal divisions.

85

Essential Unity of Religious Teachings

'All major religious traditions carry the same essential message: The importance of love, compassion, forgiveness, and tolerance. The differences in philosophical approach are secondary to these shared ethical teachings.'

Reflection

Many paths wind upward—
some steep and stony,
others shaded and slow.
Each offers its own rhythm,
its own teachings
etched into the earth.
But at the summit,
there are no signposts,
only sky—
and a stillness wide enough
to hold every traveller's story.
What mattered was not the route,
but the walking—
the breath taken,
the burden set down,
the view earned
by presence.

Meditation

Reflect on the universal ethical values—compassion, honesty, generosity, forgiveness—that appear in traditions across the world. Consider examples from various religions that express these values, whether through sacred stories, the lives of saints, or acts of kindness. Contemplate how this common ground might inspire respect and collaboration, even amidst doctrinal differences. Recognising this shared moral core can open pathways for unity without requiring agreement in belief.

86

Respecting Differences

'Sometimes people misunderstand the concept of religious harmony, thinking it requires everyone to become the same. This is not so. Mutual respect creates harmony, respecting the essential message underlying all traditions.'

Reflection

The garden does not demand
that roses become lilies,
or oak trees transform into maples.
Its harmony lies in each plant
fully expressing its unique nature
while contributing to the whole.
So, too, with faith traditions—
distinct voices singing different notes
that together create a chorus
more beautiful and complete
than any single melody alone.

Meditation

Reflect on how different spiritual traditions meet various human needs—emotional, philosophical, ritual, or communal. Think of your own path—what drew you to it, what it offers you—and imagine someone else finding equal resonance in a different path. Visualise a tapestry where each tradition is a distinct thread, contributing to the larger pattern of human wisdom. Let this awareness deepen your appreciation for religious diversity not as a threat, but as a source of collective richness.

87
Dialogue for Mutual Enrichment

'The purpose of dialogue between different religious traditions is not to create a single faith but to learn from each other while respecting differences. Like many rivers flowing to the same ocean.'

Reflection

The jewel turns in light,
each facet catching
a different glimmer of truth.
No single angle reveals
its full radiance—
yet without anyone,
the brilliance is diminished.
So it is with wisdom—
many traditions,
many tongues,
each a voice in the great chorus
echoing one ancient silence.
Not fragments,
but reflections—
each necessary,
each sacred.

Meditation

Think of a spiritual tradition different from your own. Identify one aspect of it—a teaching, ritual, or ethic—that you admire. Reflect on how this element might complement your path. Let admiration replace resistance. Imagine meeting someone from that tradition. What qualities would foster real exchange? Now reflect on how dialogue, when approached in this spirit, becomes a shared search for truth—not a competition of ideas, but a convergence of hearts.

88
Beyond Conversion to Conversation

'We do not need to convert others to our beliefs. It is excellent if someone is already ethically oriented and finds meaning in their tradition. If they are interested in Buddhism, I am happy to share. The important thing is sincere spiritual practice, not outer labels.'

Reflection

Labels tell us nothing
about the contents of the heart.
The sincere Christian, Muslim, Jew,
Hindu, or secular humanist
who embodies compassion in action
walks the same essential path
as the sincere Buddhist.
Different vehicles, same direction.
Different languages, same meaning.
The river of genuine spirituality
flows beyond the banks
of any single tradition.

Meditation

Reflect on what qualities matter most in your own spiritual life—perhaps integrity, kindness, inner peace. Now consider how those same qualities manifest in traditions different from your own. Let their expressions inspire rather than challenge you. Contemplate the difference between religious identification and lived spiritual depth. Let your motivation shift from convincing others to understanding and appreciating sincere practice in all its forms.

89
Harmony through Shared Values

'Religious harmony doesn't come from theological agreement but from recognising our shared human values. When people of different faiths work together on issues like peace, justice, and environmental protection, differences in belief become less divisive.'

Reflection

Above the doctrines that divide,
beneath the rituals that distinguish,
runs a current of shared concern:
For the child who hungers,
for the land that withers,
for communities torn by violence.
In the space of common action,
hands reach across ancient boundaries,
not by abandoning conviction,
but by embodying its deepest truth:
Compassion that transcends category,
service that speaks a universal tongue.

Meditation

Identify a global or local issue—perhaps hunger, injustice, or climate change. Consider how people of diverse faiths address this concern, each guided by their ethical teachings. Reflect on how collaboration rooted in shared values brings strength, transcending doctrinal differences. Contemplate how your own tradition calls you to serve—and how this service unites rather than divides across beliefs.

90
Finding Wisdom in Different Paths

'Dialogue is not about converting others to our view but about mutual enrichment. Each tradition has unique insights and methods that can complement others' understanding. This exchange requires deep listening and humility.'

Reflection

Not the marketplace of competing products,
but the roundtable of shared wisdom.
Not the battlefield of contradicting claims,
but the garden where diverse seeds
cross-pollinate to create
new, unexpected beauty.
True dialogue asks not
'Who is right?'
but 'What can we learn
from each other's truth?'

Meditation

Think of a tradition or philosophy different from your own. Without analysing, ask: 'What might I learn here?' Acknowledge any resistance that arises. Let humility soften it. Contemplate how true dialogue arises not from certainty, but from shared inquiry. Let yourself be taught—by difference, not despite it, but because of it.

Chapter 16

Environmental Ethics

The Dalai Lama has long been a powerful voice for environmental protection, connecting Buddhist principles of interdependence and compassion with urgent ecological concerns. His approach to environmental ethics emerges not from political ideology but from a profound understanding of our interconnection with the natural world and responsibility towards future generations.

In Buddhist philosophy, humans are not separate from nature but integral parts of a vast interdependent web. This perspective naturally extends ethical concern beyond human society, including all living beings and the ecosystems that sustain them. The Dalai Lama emphasises that environmental protection is not merely a technical issue but a moral and spiritual one, requiring a fundamental shift in how we perceive our relationship with the natural world.

This chapter explores how traditional Buddhist values provide a foundation for responding to contemporary environmental challenges. We examine how the principle of interdependence illuminates our profound connections with ecological systems, how compassion naturally extends to non-human beings, and how simplicity and contentment offer alternatives to the excessive consumption driving environmental degradation.

The Dalai Lama teaches that genuine environmental ethics must balance pragmatic action with inner transformation—addressing immediate crises while cultivating the wisdom and compassion that support sustainable, harmonious relationships with our planet. Through this integrated approach, care for the Earth becomes not an obligation to be shouldered but a natural expression of our deepest values.

91
Interdependence with the Natural World

'The concept of interdependence reminds us that humans are not separate from nature but part of an intricate web of life. What we do to the environment, we ultimately do to ourselves, since we depend entirely on the Earth's systems for our survival and well-being.'

Reflection

The air in my lungs
was yesterday's gift from forests.
The water in my cells
has cycled through countless forms.
The elements of my body
once danced in distant stars.
There is no boundary
where 'I' end and 'nature' begins—
only relationship so intimate
we've forgotten its existence,
like fish unaware of water
until it begins to disappear.

Meditation

Begin by gently observing your breath. Reflect on how each inhalation connects you to forests, oceans, and weather systems that sustain the air. Turn your awareness to thewater in your body—its long journey through clouds, rivers, animals, and plants before reaching you. Consider your food. Trace it back through farms, soil, rainfall, sunshine, and unseen life forms. Finally, contemplate how climate, biodiversity, and natural cycles make your life possible Recognise this intricate web of dependence with humility and care.

92

Extending Compassion to All Beings

'Our circle of compassion must extend beyond humans to include animals and ecosystems. When we recognise that all sentient beings seek to avoid suffering just as we do, environmental protection becomes a practical necessity and a moral imperative.'

Reflection

The bird's desire to feed its young,
the fish's struggle against the current,
the forest's slow reach towards light—
all expressions of the same life force
that moves through my own veins.
What strange amnesia allows us
to separate ourselves from this family,
to draw the circle of concern so small
it excludes our very kin,
the beings whose existence
makes our own possible?

Meditation

Begin by connecting with your own wish to be happy and free from suffering. Feel this wish sincerely in your heart. Now expand this awareness to include others—your loved ones, strangers, even those you find difficult. Gradually include animals—those you know and those you don't—recognising their vulnerability and desire for well-being. Finally, extend this compassion to forests, rivers, and coral reefs—entire living systems. Allow your heart to open to their beauty and fragility.

93

Simple Living and Contentment

'Environmental problems are largely driven by excessive consumption—wanting more than we need. The practice of contentment, finding satisfaction with enough rather than constantly craving more, offers both personal happiness and a sustainable relationship with our planet.'

Reflection

The hungry ghost feeds
on what it cannot hold—
each craving fulfilled
only sharpens the ache.
More becomes less,
and satisfaction slips
like water through fingers.
But contentment lays a humble table,
sets a bowl of sunlight and silence,
a cup of breath and presence.
It gathers no excess,
yet nothing is missing.
What was once soul wisdom
now speaks to soil and sky—
a teaching not only to soothe the mind,
but to heal the Earth itself.

Meditation

Consider contentment as a form of ecological awareness. Reflect on what 'enough' means in your own life—not as deprivation, but as clarity. Distinguish between needs and wants. What truly sustains your well-being? Observe how cravings and habits influence your consumption. Now bring to mind the deep fulfilment you've found in simplicity—perhaps through time in nature, connection, service, or creativity. Let these memories anchor your sense of sufficiency.

94
Environmental Justice

'Environmental challenges affect the most vulnerable first and most severely. A compassionate response requires protecting nature in the abstract and ensuring that environmental benefits and burdens are shared fairly, with special concern for those most at risk.'

Reflection

The hurricane does not strike all roofs alike,
nor does the drought steal water from every well.
Where power pools and privilege shelters,
the wounds of the Earth run deeper elsewhere.
The fault lines are not only in the soil
but in our systems—
where profit speaks louder than prayer,
and convenience drowns out care.
To tend the Earth
is to tend its people,
especially those unheard,
whose suffering lies hidden beneath
the noise of short-term gain.
True healing begins
where justice meets compassion—
rooted in the truth
that the planet and its people
are not separate,
but one breath,
shared.

Meditation

Consider how access to clean air, safe water, and natural spaces often reflects privilege. Reflect on the communities most affected by climate change and pollution. What responsibilities come with your own access and influence? Let this awareness inspire compassion rooted in fairness, not guilt.

95

Balancing Pragmatism and Vision

'Environmental action requires both pragmatic steps that address immediate problems and a long-term vision of harmony between humans and nature. Neither alone is sufficient—we need practical solutions guided by compassionate wisdom.'

Reflection

The healer tends not only
to the fever's flare,
but to the hidden disharmony
beneath the skin.
The gardener does not stop
at chasing pests—
she nourishes the soil
for seasons yet to come.
So, too, must we learn
to act across time's vast weave:
to build shelter
against today's howling wind,
even as we plant
the quiet seeds of tomorrow's forest—
roots we may never see,
canopies we may never rest beneath,
but whose shade we must still imagine
into being.

Meditation

Bring to mind an environmental issue you care about. Identify one concrete action you can take now to reduce harm. Then step back—what more profound shift in values, systems, or awareness would address the root cause? Let your motivation be grounded in both immediacy and imagination. These are not opposites but partners in healing.

96
Hope and Resilience

'Environmental challenges can seem overwhelming, leading to despair or denial. However, both Buddhist practice and ecological understanding teach us that change is always possible. Cultivating hope based on reality rather than wishful thinking gives us resilience for the work ahead.'

Reflection

Hope is not naive optimism
that ignores the flames,
nor is it the despair
that abandons the burning house.
Hope is the clear-eyed courage
that grabs the bucket,
calls to neighbours,
and begins the work of dousing
even as the fire rages.
It draws strength not from certainty of outcome
but from certainty of purpose,
from knowing that each drop matters
in ways we may never fully see.

Meditation

Acknowledge the pain and urgency of environmental decline. Let your heart open without collapsing. Now bring to mind moments of recovery—ecosystems healed, communities united, lives renewed. What helps you stay engaged even when the future is uncertain? Remember your values, your capacity, and the collective potential for renewal. Let hope arise not from denial, but from love in action.

Chapter 17

Integrating Wisdom and Compassion in Daily Life

IN THIS BOOK, WE HAVE EXPLORED VARIOUS ASPECTS OF the Dalai Lama's teachings—from mindfulness and emotional awareness to wisdom, compassion, and ethical living. While examining these elements individually helps us understand them clearly, in practice, they function together as an integrated whole, much like the systems of the body that support and enhance one another.

This chapter explores how the teachings we've discussed integrate into daily life. The Dalai Lama emphasises that genuine spiritual practice is intertwined with our ordinary experiences. This connection allows our meditation to enhance our interactions, deepen our compassion through wisdom, and guide our ethical choices towards greater clarity and peace.

Mindfulness lays the groundwork for emotional transformation, cultivating awareness and creating space for wisdom to develop. As wisdom grows, true compassion emerges, leading to ethical actions that benefit everyone. This growth cycle is self-reinforcing, with advancements in one area supporting progress in others.

We learn to cultivate a unified approach in which wisdom and compassion, meditation and action, inner work and outer engagement become different expressions of the same integrated understanding.

Through this holistic perspective, we transcend the division between spiritual practice and ordinary life. Every interaction becomes an opportunity for mindfulness, every challenge an invitation to apply wisdom, and every relationship a context for compassion. Thus, daily life transforms into the very path of practice, becoming its most essential expression.

97

The Inseparability of Wisdom and Compassion

'Compassion without wisdom is incomplete, while wisdom without compassion remains sterile. These two qualities must be developed together, like the two wings of a bird needing each other for flight.'

Reflection

Clarity alone cuts clean—
but leaves the wound exposed.
Compassion alone embraces—
but may lose its way in the shadow.
The eye that sees truly,
and the heart that feels deeply,
must move as one.
Like wings of a bird,
they rise only together—
vision and love,
direction and warmth—
the full gesture
of awakening made whole.

Meditation

Reflect on impermanence and interdependence—how all things, including yourself, arise from countless conditions and are in constant flux. Notice how this brings perspective. From this wisdom, let compassion arise naturally, opening your heart to the struggles of others. Remember that wisdom without compassion can lead to detachment, and compassion without wisdom can be draining. Consider a situation in your life that could benefit from both clarity and kindness, allowing these qualities to guide your response.

98
Meditation and Action

'Formal meditation and daily activity are not separate spheres but complementary aspects of spiritual development. Meditation cultivates qualities that inform our actions, while mindful engagement with life provides the testing ground for our practice.'

Reflection

The dance between stillness and movement,
between silence and speech,
between inward gaze and outward service—
this is the rhythm of genuine awakening.
The mountain stream that pools in quiet depths
then flows onward with renewed strength.
The breath that draws inward for nourishment
then extends outward in expression.
No division between sacred and ordinary—
only the seamless flow of presence
through all dimensions of living.

Meditation

Begin with a few minutes of calm, focused breathing. Then reflect on how the qualities meditation nurtures—such as clarity, openness, and compassion—can shape your interactions, tasks, and speech. Finally, reverse the lens: How do the demands and relationships of daily life deepen your practice? How do they reveal your growing edges? Let the feedback between these spheres create an integrated path of development.

99
Inner Transformation and Outer Engagement

'Inner development and social responsibility
are not opposed but complementary.
The deeper our inner transformation, the more
effective our contribution to society becomes.
And engagement with the world's challenges
deepens our spiritual understanding.'

Reflection

The tree thrives in two directions—
roots sinking deep into shadowed earth,
branches lifting into radiant sky.
Sever one, and the other withers.
So, too, the human spirit—
drawn inward toward stillness,
outward towards service.
Not rivals, but reflections
of the same sacred impulse
to grow, to offer, to become.
True flourishing arises
when silence nourishes action,
and action flows from depth—
a life whole, rooted, and reaching.

Meditation

Reflect on how inner work and external service are linked. Notice how qualities like awareness, emotional balance, and compassion make you more skilful in the world. Then consider how everyday engagements—challenges, relationships, tasks—highlight where more inner growth is needed. Let your practice and life become mirrors to each other, deepening the other in an ongoing exchange.

100
Ethics as Natural Expression

'When wisdom and compassion mature,
ethical conduct becomes less about following
rules and more a natural expression of our deepest
understanding. We avoid harmful actions not
from fear of consequences but from seeing their
incompatibility with our true nature.'

Reflection

The child learns by listening—
what to touch, what to avoid.
The adolescent pushes—
testing walls to find their shape.
But true maturity is not rebellion
nor obedience—
it is alignment.
A quiet knowing
that needs no command.
Like water flowing downhill,
like sunlight warming without effort,
ethics arise not from fear,
but from inner coherence—
not imposed,
but embodied.

Meditation

From external rules, to reasoning, to heartfelt intuition—observe your current relationship with right action. Recall moments when ethical choices felt like a struggle, and others when they emerged effortlessly from clarity and care. Notice the difference in those experiences. Now bring to mind an ethical challenge you face. Instead of debating it, ask: 'What choice most expresses my deepest values?'

101

Wholeness in Relationships

'Our spiritual practice and relationship with others are not separate domains. The same awareness, wisdom, and compassion we cultivate in meditation naturally express themselves in listening, speaking, and responding to those around us.'

Reflection

There is no true divide
between the one who sits in stillness
and the one who speaks with care,
between the one who contemplates emptiness
and the one who holds a friend's grief.
Reading sacred texts,
mending broken trust—
each arises from the same heart-mind,
each sings a different octave
of the same unstruck chord.
The boundary between sacred and ordinary
is drawn only by forgetfulness.
In truth, every encounter—
every gesture of presence—is lit from within.
All relationship is holy ground.

Meditation

Reflect on how qualities from your practice—such as mindfulness, compassion, patience—might be more consciously brought into your interactions with them. Notice how your relationships reveal your inner patterns—defensiveness, impatience, care, love—and how these patterns can be worked with just as you would in formal meditation. Let each relationship become a place of eal-time spiritual practice.

102
Joy in the Integrated Path

'When wisdom, compassion, and mindfulness begin to work together harmoniously, a natural joy arises. This is not dependent on perfect circumstances but emerges from the very process of integration itself, a happiness born of wholeness rather than fragmentation.'

Reflection

A symphony blooms into fullness
when every instrument finds its voice—
not in rivalry,
but in resonance.
Each note deepens the whole,
each silence holds the song.
So it is in practice—
when mindfulness steadies,
wisdom clarifies,
compassion warms,
and ethics ground.
No single virtue stands alone;
together they weave
the quiet harmony of being.
Joy is not a separate prize—
but the music that arises
when we are finally
in tune
with ourselves.

Meditation

Turn your attention to the qualities you've developed: Mindfulness, insight, compassion, ethical conduct. Feel how they work together, supporting and enriching one another. Notice how this integration itself gives rise to a quiet joy—not based on external success, but on inner harmony. Let this joy deepen as you rest in the awareness of being whole.

Chapter 18

The Journey of Transformation

THE PATH OF INNER TRANSFORMATION IS NOT A STRAIGHT line but a journey with its own rhythm, challenges, and unexpected discoveries. The Dalai Lama often emphasises that genuine spiritual development happens gradually over time, like a tree's slow but steady growth. While we may experience dramatic insights or breakthroughs along the way, lasting transformation emerges from consistent practice and patient engagement with life's experiences.

This chapter explores the nature of the transformative journey—how to approach it with dedication and gentleness, work with obstacles, and recognise authentic progress beyond superficial changes. The Dalai Lama teaches that this journey is not about becoming someone different but about uncovering our true nature, which has been obscured by confusion and habitual patterns.

We begin by examining the importance of starting where we are—accepting our current conditions with honesty while maintaining aspiration for growth. We then explore the role of effort and patience, finding the middle way between complacent passivity and straining impatience. The Dalai Lama guides us in working with the inevitable obstacles and setbacks that arise, showing how these challenges become opportunities for deeper learning when approached with wisdom.

As we conclude our exploration of these 108 teachings, we come to appreciate that the journey of transformation has no final destination but continues to unfold throughout our lives. Each step on the path brings its own fulfilment, and the qualities we develop along the way—mindfulness, wisdom, compassion, and joy—are both the means of transformation and its natural expression.

103

Beginning Where We Are

'Spiritual practice begins with the courage to see ourselves clearly—to acknowledge our light and our shadow, wisdom and wounds. From this honest recognition, coupled with a heartfelt aspiration to grow, arises the true foundation upon which the inner journey rests.'

Reflection

The wise gardener does not scold the soil
for being dry or dense.
She studies it with quiet attention—
noticing its texture, its thirst,
its readiness to nourish life.
She begins where she is,
not where she wishes to be.
And with care, patience, and vision,
she coaxes forth what might bloom.
So, too, on the inner path—
transformation begins
not with judgement or illusion,
but with clear-eyed honesty
and the gentle fire of aspiration.
We root ourselves in what is,
even as we lean
towards what may yet become.

Meditation

Acknowledge both the strengths you have cultivated and the areas where you struggle. Allow yourself to see clearly—without exaggeration or denial—where you are on the path. Notice if the mind veers towards self-judgement or complacency. Can you meet your situation with honesty and warmth? Now connect with your aspiration—not as a form of rejection, but as a natural extension of self-respect. What qualities would you like to nurture? Which patterns would you like to soften? Feel the quiet dignity of being both truthful and aspiring. Let this become the ground for your ongoing practice.

104
Effort and Patience

'Inner transformation requires both diligent effort and patient acceptance. Too much striving creates tension and frustration, while too little effort leads to complacency. Finding the middle way between these extremes is itself a crucial practice.'

106

Recognising Authentic Progress

'True spiritual progress often appears not in ramatic experiences but in subtle shifts in how we respond to daily situations. Decreasing reactivity, growing patience with difficulties, and greater cern for others' welfare are more reliable signs of nsformation than temporary emotional states.'

Reflection

The farmer knows—
no amount of tugging
will hasten the seedling's rise.
Growth follows its own rhythm,
unfolding in quiet partnership
with sun, soil, and time.
Yet neglect bears no harvest.
Without water, watchfulness,
and patient tending,
even the most fertile seed
withers unseen.
So, too, with the inner life—
we walk a middle path:
Devoted, yet unforced;
intentional, yet unhurried.
Honouring both the effort we make
and the mystery that moves through us.

Meditation

Reflect on an area where you may be pushing too hard for quick results, feeling frustrated by slow progress. Notice this tension in your body and mind, then soften—allow your breath and awareness to return. Consider where you might be putting in too little effort, perhaps avoiding depth. How can you refresh your intention without strain? Seek a balanced path: Steady, sincere, patient, and spacious. Let this balance settle in your breath and awareness.

105

Working with Obstacles

'Obstacles on the spiritual path—whether external difficulties or internal resistances—are not failures but opportunities for deeper learning. When approached with wisdom, these very challenges become catalysts for growth.'

Reflection

The tallest trees do not rise
in tranquil valleys,
but cling to windswept ridges,
where storms carve character
into every limb.
Their roots drive deep
not despite the gale,
but because of it—
each blast a tutor in resilience,
each winter a lesson in grace.
So, too, with us.
The obstacles we resist,
the tensions we fear,
may hold the seeds of strength.
Met with presence,
challenges do not break us—
they shape us,
revealing depths
we would never have found
in softer soil.

Meditation

Think of an obstacle you're fa
relationships, or emotions. Instead
what it might reveal. What insig
engaging with it mindfully?
reactions and soften your
challenge that led to growth
see your current difficulty as a

Reflection

The young tree's growth
is imperceptible day to day,
visible only to those who mark its height
over months and seasons.
So, too, with inner development—
not measured in moments of ecstasy
or sudden revelation,
but in the quiet evidence of daily living:
The sharper word not spoken,
the grudge not nursed,
the helping hand extended,
the judgement withheld,
the calm maintained amid chaos—
small gestures that reveal
the profound shifts beneath.

Meditation

Sit quietly and recall how you've typically measured spiritual progress. Has it been through extraordinary experiences or emotional highs? Now, turn your attention to subtler signs: Have you become less reactive? More compassionate? Quicker to return to presence? Reflect on recent situations where you may have acted or responded differently than in the past. Let yourself appreciate these quiet shifts—not with pride, but with a grateful awareness of transformation unfolding gently over time.

107
The Path as Continuous Unfolding

'There is no final destination in spiritual development, no point where we can say "now I am complete". Rather, the path continues to unfold throughout our lives, with each stage revealing new dimensions of understanding and practice.'

Reflection

The horizon we walked towards yesterday
becomes the ground beneath our feet today,
revealing a new horizon ahead.
The question that consumed us for years
finds its answer, which then opens
ten more questions previously unimagined.
The path spirals upward and inward simultaneously,
returning to familiar territory
but always at a different level,
each cycle, both completion and beginning,
each arrival a new departure,
the journey itself, both means and end—
one continuous unfolding without conclusion.

Meditation

Take time to reflect on the evolving nature of your spiritual journey. Recall an insight or understanding that once felt complete but later opened into something more nuanced. Reflect on teachings or practices that have deepened in meaning over time. Notice how questions often lead not to final answers, but to richer inquiries. Allow this reflection to open a sense of humility and wonder. Rather than striving for a fixed goal, rest in the unfolding rhythm, each step revealing new terrain.

108

Joy in the Journey

'The journey of transformation is not merely a means to future happiness but contains its own joy in each step. When we recognise that each moment of practice is itself the expression of our Buddha nature, we discover happiness not as a distant goal but as inherent in the very process of awakening.'

Reflection

The child climbing the mountain
asks repeatedly, 'Are we there yet?'
focused only on the distant peak.
The seasoned climber knows
the summit is but one moment
in the fullness of the journey—
each step, each breath, each vista along the way
complete in itself, lacking nothing.
So, too, on the spiritual path,
where awakening is not postponed to the future
but discovered anew with each mindful step,
each compassionate act, each moment of clarity,
the journey and destination inseparable,
like wave and water, sun and light.

Meditation

Sit with the intention of practising for the sake of the present moment—not to reach a future state, but simply to be here, now. Release the notion of progress or results. Instead, feel the natural joy of presence: The ease of the breath, the stillness of sitting, the intimacy with your own experience. Recall a moment when practising felt nourishing or quietly fulfilling—how that joy arose not from attainment but from awareness itself. Let the simplicity of being present become its own reward.

Glossary of Key Terms with Chapter References

Afflictive Emotions

Disturbing mental states such as anger, attachment, jealousy, and pride obscure clarity and give rise to suffering. His Holiness teaches that transformation—not suppression—of these emotions is the path to freedom.

Referenced in: Chapter 18

Analytical Meditation

A form of meditation that uses reasoned reflection and inquiry to examine the nature of reality or a specific theme. It contrasts with stabilising meditation, which cultivates calm concentration by actively engaging the intellect to develop insight.

Referenced in: Chapters 13, 18, 3, 5

Appreciative Joy

Taking genuine delight in the happiness and success of others. One of the Four Immeasurables, this quality counters envy and supports open-heartedness.

Referenced in: Chapters 12, 18

Awareness

The non-dual, luminous knowing that underlies all mental activity. In advanced Buddhist practice, awareness (rigpa) directly recognises the mind's true nature.

Referenced in: Chapter 7

Bodhisattva

A being who seeks enlightenment not only for their own liberation but to aid all sentient beings. The Dalai Lama is revered as a living Bodhisattva who embodies this altruistic ideal.

Referenced in: Chapter 18

Buddha Nature

The innate potential for awakening exists within all beings. It is not something acquired but uncovered through spiritual practice—our fundamental nature, luminous and untainted.

Referenced in: Chapter 18

Compassion

The heartfelt wish that others be free from suffering and its causes. It arises from recognising shared vulnerability and is expressed through courageous, wise, and caring action. His Holiness often emphasises compassion as the most important spiritual value and the foundation of a meaningful life.

Referenced in: Chapters 1, 3, 6, 7, 10, 11, 13, 14, 15, 17, 18

Concentration

A steady, unwavering focus of attention on a chosen object, developed through stabilising (śamatha) meditation. It serves as the foundation for insight and transformation.

Referenced in: Chapters 13, 18

Contentment

A sense of inner sufficiency and gratitude for what is present. Contentment softens craving and fosters peace—a recurring theme in His Holiness's teachings on happiness.

Referenced in: Chapter 16

Direct Experience

A level of knowing that transcends intellectual analysis. Direct experience, particularly through meditation, reveals truth as lived insight, not merely conceptual understanding.

Referenced in: Chapters 14, 18, 3, 5

Eight Worldly Concerns

The four pairs of hope and fear that bind us to suffering: gain/loss, pleasure/pain, praise/blame, and fame/disgrace. Freedom from these concerns is a mark of spiritual maturity.

Referenced in: Chapter 18

Emptiness (*Śūnyatā*)
The insight that phenomena do not exist independently or inherently. Instead, all things arise in dependence on causes, conditions, and conceptual labels. Far from nihilism, it opens the mind to freedom and the heart to compassion.
Referenced in: Chapters 11, 14, 17, 18, 6

Equanimity
A balanced mind free of bias, enabling us to meet all beings with impartial care. It is foundational to mature love and compassion.
Referenced in: Chapters 10, 12, 18

Ethical Conduct
The basis of all spiritual practice. It includes right speech, action, and livelihood—guided by compassion and the wish to reduce harm.
Referenced in: Chapters 11, 17, 18

Four Noble Truths
The Buddha's foundational teaching: (1) There is suffering. (2) It has causes. (3) It can end. (4) There is a path to its cessation—ethical living, meditation, and wisdom.
Referenced in: Chapter 18

Freedom
Not simply external liberty, but inner release from afflictive emotions, ignorance, and reactive patterns. The goal of spiritual practice is inner freedom.
Referenced in: Chapter 18

Happiness (*Sukha*)
As defined by the Dalai Lama, happiness is inner peace grounded in warm-heartedness, ethical living, and wisdom. It is cultivated rather than found and is distinct from fleeting pleasure.
Referenced in: Chapter 12

Hope
For His Holiness, hope is not naïve optimism but a realistic, grounded confidence rooted in ethical action and a sense of universal responsibility.
Referenced in: Chapter 16

Impermanence (Anitya)
The truth that all conditioned things are constantly changing, arising, and passing away. Reflecting on impermanence helps release grasping and enhances appreciation of the present moment.
Referenced in: Chapters 12, 18

Inner Transformation
The gradual reshaping of one's thoughts, habits, and responses through ethical living, meditation, and insight. Central to His Holiness's vision of spiritual growth.
Referenced in: Chapter 18

Interdependence (Pratītyasamutpāda)
The view that all things arise in dependence upon other causes, conditions, and concepts. Realising this dissolves self-centredness and promotes empathy.
Referenced in: Chapters 16, 6

Joy
A stable inner state rooted in peace, ethical integrity, and compassion—not fleeting pleasure. His Holiness embodies this quality as a mark of spiritual maturity.
Referenced in: Chapters 12, 18

Karma
The principle of ethical cause and effect: every intention and action imprints consciousness and shapes future experience. Karma empowers responsibility.
Referenced in: Chapter 18

Levels of Understanding
His Holiness teaches three levels: (1) learning from others, (2) reasoning for oneself, and (3) direct meditative insight. These deepen progressively through study and practice.
Referenced in: Chapters 14, 2, 5

Liberation (*Nirvāna*)
Freedom from suffering and cyclic existence (samsāra*)* is achieved through the realisation of emptiness and the cessation of ignorance and afflictions.
Referenced in: Chapter 18

Love (*Maitrī*)
The wish for others to be happy—unconditional and free of attachment. It differs from romantic or possessive love and is cultivated as an expansive inner quality.
Referenced in: Chapters 12, 7, 8

Meditation
The disciplined training of the mind. Includes stabilising (*śamatha*) to build focus and analytical (*vipaśyanā*) to cultivate insight. Central to transformation in all traditions.
Referenced in: Chapters 13, 18, 3, 5

Mental Afflictions (*Kleśa*)
Obscuring mental states that distort perception and give ise to suffering. These include the three poisons and countless subtle distortions.
Referenced in: Chapter 18

Middle Way
A philosophical and practical path that avoids extremes—between indulgence and austerity, or eternalism and nihilism. It underpins His Holiness's entire outlook.
Referenced in: Chapter 5

Mindfulness (*Smiti*)
The capacity to sustain attention and remember the object of focus. For His Holiness, it includes ethical vigilance—monitoring the quality of the mind moment by moment.
Referenced in: Chapters 13, 18, 3

Neuroplasticity
The scientific recognition that the brain changes with experience, particularly intentional training such as meditation. His Holiness cites this to bridge science and dharma.
Referenced in: Chapter 14

Non-violence (*Ahimsa*)
A deep commitment not to harm others in thought, word, or action. Rooted in compassion and courage, it is central to His Holiness's political and spiritual philosophy.
Referenced in: Chapter 16

Perspective / Interpretation
His Holiness often teaches that suffering is shaped not just by events but by our interpretation of them. Shifting perspective can transform how we experience adversity.
Referenced in: Chapters 17, 7

Prayer Beads (*Mālā*)
A string of 108 beads used to count recitations of mantras or prayers. Symbolises purification of the 108 defilements in Buddhist practice.
Referenced in: Chapter 13

Realistic Compassion
A mature, discerning form of compassion that includes wise boundaries and avoids burnout. For His Holiness, genuine compassion must be sustainable and anchored in wisdom.
Referenced in: Chapter 17

Refuge
Seeking shelter in the Buddha (teacher), Dharma (teaching), and Sangha (spiritual community). In a secular sense, it means grounding one's life in wisdom and compassion.
Referenced in: Chapters 1, 18

Secular Ethics
Ethical values such as compassion, honesty, and non-violence are universal and not based on religion. Central to His Holiness's vision for global peace and coexistence.
Referenced in: Chapters 14, 15

Self-Compassion
Extending kindness to oneself during difficulty or failure, as one would to a loved one. Without it, compassion for others becomes unsustainable.
Referenced in: Chapter 17

Spiritual Materialism
The use of spiritual practice to reinforce ego or self-importance. His Holiness warns against using dharma as a badge of identity rather than as a path to transformation.
Referenced in: Chapter 13

Stabilising Meditation (*Śamatha*)
Cultivating a calm, clear, focused mind through sustained attention. It prepares the ground for insight.
Referenced in: Chapters 13, 18, 5

Suffering (*Duhkha*)
The unsatisfactoriness of life when ruled by craving, aversion, and ignorance. Recognising suffering is the first step on the path to liberation.
Referenced in: Chapters 18, 4

The Three Poisons
Ignorance, attachment, and aversion—the root causes of all suffering in Buddhism. All harmful thoughts and actions stem from these.
Referenced in: Chapter 18

Tonglen
A Tibetan meditation of 'giving and taking.' One breathes in others' suffering and breathes out relief. This practice builds courage and compassion.
Referenced in: Chapter 6

Universal Responsibility
A core theme in His Holiness's teaching is that every person shares responsibility for the happiness and welfare of others and the planet.
Referenced in: Chapters 15, 16

Virtue (*Kuśala*)
Positive mental qualities such as patience, generosity, and truthfulness. These are the building blocks of happiness and inner freedom.
Referenced in: Chapter 11

Wisdom (*Prajñā*)
The insight into the true nature of reality—impermanence, emptiness, and interdependence. Wisdom must always be coupled with compassion to liberate.
Referenced in: Chapter 14

Thematic Practice Plans

These seven-day practice sequences are designed to help you deeply explore specific themes. Each path builds progressively, allowing you to develop understanding and skill through consistent practice. You can follow these paths at your own pace, spending more than one day on a practice if needed, or return to them repeatedly to deepen your experience.

1. Seven-Day Path: Cultivating Compassion

Day 1: Foundation of Shared Aspiration

Practice: For fifteen minutes, reflect on how your desire for happiness and freedom from suffering connects you to all living beings. Begin with yourself, acknowledging your natural wish to be happy, then gradually extend this recognition to loved ones, acquaintances, strangers, and finally, all beings.

Quote: 'Everyone seeks happiness and wishes to avoid suffering. This is not just a human desire but the fundamental nature of all sentient beings. Understanding this universal aspiration creates a natural foundation for compassion.' (Chapter 1)

Day 2: Self-Compassion

Practice: When you observe an area of struggle or self-criticism today, pause to offer yourself the same kindness you would offer a dear friend facing the same difficulty. Place a hand on your heart and acknowledge: 'This is difficult. This is part of being human. May I be kind to myself in this struggle.'

Quote: 'Self-compassion is the foundation for compassion toward others. If we cannot meet our own suffering with kindness, our compassion for others will be limited and eventually exhausted.' (Chapter 7)

Day 3: Compassionate Understanding

Practice: When someone behaves in a difficult way today, pause to consider what suffering or confusion might be driving their actions. Without excusing harmful behaviour, practise seeing the vulnerable human being behind the behaviour—someone who, like you, wishes to be happy but may be caught in unskilful patterns.

Quote: 'In dealing with difficult people, remember that their harmful behaviour arises from their own suffering and confused thinking. This doesn't excuse their actions but helps us respond with composure rather than escalating hostility.' (Chapter 8)

Day 4: Widening the Circle

Practice: Today, consciously extend your circle of care beyond those closest to you. When reading news or moving through public spaces, remind yourself that each person you encounter or read about shares the same wish for happiness and freedom from suffering as you do. Observe how this recognition affects your sense of connection.

Quote: 'The essence of spiritual practice is to diminish self-centredness and expand our circle of concern. As we do this, we discover that our own happiness is intimately connected to the well-being of others.' (Chapter 10)

Day 5: Balanced Compassion

Practice: When you feel moved to help someone today, engage your heart and mind. Ask yourself two questions: 'What is the compassionate wish here?' and 'What is the wisest response?' Observe how these two aspects inform and balance each other.

Quote: 'Our view of compassion is often too sentimental. True compassion includes warmth and wisdom—the courage to witness suffering and the wisdom to respond skilfully rather than reactively.' (Chapter 6)

Day 6: Tonglen Practice

Practice: For fifteen minutes, practise tonglen. With each in-breath, visualise taking in the suffering of a specific person or group as a dark cloud. With each out-breath, send light, relief, and healing—offering whatever would bring them happiness and well-being. Observe how this practice challenges our habitual tendency to avoid others' pain.

Quote: 'The practice of tonglen—taking in others' suffering and sending out relief—demonstrates the transformative power of compassion. Instead of avoiding others' pain, we willingly connect with it, discovering that this connection transforms ourselves and others.' (Chapter 6)

Day 7: Compassion and Emptiness

Practice: For twenty minutes, contemplate how your existence depends on others and how your actions affect others' well-being. Consider: If we truly exist interdependently, what happens to the sharp boundary between 'my suffering' and 'your suffering'? Between 'my happiness' and 'your happiness'?

Quote: 'When we truly understand emptiness—the lack of inherent, independent existence in all phenomena—compassion arises naturally. Seeing that all beings exist interdependently, their suffering and well-being become inseparable from our own.' (Chapter 6)

2. Seven-Day Path: Working with Difficult Emotions

Day 1: Creating Space Around Emotions
Practice: When a difficult emotion arises today, practise the three-step process: 1) Recognise it ('This is anger'); 2) Accept its presence without judgement; 3) Investigate it with curiosity—its physical sensations, the thoughts feeding it, its changing quality. Observe how this approach differs from either suppressing or being swept away by the emotion.

Quote: 'The key to transforming negative emotions is mindful awareness, not suppression or indulgence. By clearly observing anger or desire, we create space around it and discover the freedom to respond skilfully.' (Chapter 4)

Day 2: Understanding Anger's Roots
Practice: The next time anger arises, pause before acting and silently ask yourself: 'What feels threatened right now?' Take a breath and observe if the anger is protecting something important (like a boundary or value) or just defending an image of yourself.

Quote: 'When we examine anger closely, we find it comes from feeling threatened. This threat may be to our physical safety, but more often to our self-image or cherished beliefs. Understanding this helps us respond more skilfully.' (Chapter 4)

Day 3: Transforming Fear
Practice: When fear arises today, pause and ask yourself: 'Is this fear protecting me from genuine danger, or is it protecting me from growth, connection, or necessary change?' Observe the different qualities between fears that serve you and fears that limit you.

Quote: 'Fear often masquerades as wisdom, cautioning us against taking risks or opening our hearts. Through Buddhist practice, we learn to distinguish between reasonable caution and the habitual fears that limit our potential for growth and connection.' (Chapter 4)

Day 4: Channelling Emotional Energy

Practice: When you feel a strong emotion today (especially anger), practise separating its components: the raw energy (felt in the body), the underlying caring (what value is at stake), and any hostile intention. Experiment with channelling the energy towards constructive protection of what you value, without the hostility.

Quote: 'Anger is not inherently destructive. When understood and channelled properly, its energy can fuel positive action. The key is to separate the energy of anger from the hostile intention that typically accompanies it.' (Chapter 4)

Day 5: Working with Attachment

Practice: In one important relationship today, observe moments when attachment arises—perhaps when the person doesn't respond as you'd hoped or makes a choice different from what you would prefer. Practise shifting from 'What am I getting from this relationship?' to 'What would truly support this person's happiness?'

Quote: 'Attachment is often confused with love, but they are fundamentally different. Love wishes for the other's happiness while attachment focuses on what we can get from them to secure our own happiness.' (Chapter 8)

Day 6: Addressing the Roots of Suffering

Practice: Observe when you're experiencing discontent or frustration today. Identify the expectation or 'should' creating that feeling. Then practise temporarily setting aside that expectation and meeting your actual experience with acceptance. Observe the shift in your emotional state when you close the gap between expectation and reality.

Quote: 'Much of our suffering comes from comparing our actual experience with our expectations. If we can accept reality as it is, we find a profound peace before applying our concepts of how it should be.' (Chapter 3)

Day 7: Cultivating Emotional Freedom

Practice: Throughout the day, experiment with the practice of equanimity. When pleasant experiences arise, enjoy them without grasping; when unpleasant experiences surface, acknowledge them without aversion; when neutral experiences appear, give them full attention rather than seeking stimulation. Observe how this balanced approach creates a sense of inner freedom.

Quote: 'Equanimity doesn't mean indifference. It means maintaining mental balance regardless of circumstances, allowing us to respond skilfully rather than react habitually to life's fluctuations.' (Chapter 4)

3. Seven-Day Path: Exploring Wisdom and Reality

Day 1: Understanding Interdependence

Practice: Choose any object you use daily and spend fifteen minutes tracing back all the elements that had to come together for it to exist—materials, people, knowledge, transportation systems, energy sources. Extend this web of connections as far as you can, noting how even the simplest item connects you to countless beings and processes across time and space.

Quote: 'Interdependence means that nothing exists in isolation. Every person, object, and event arises through countless causes and conditions and exists only in relation to everything else.' (Chapter 5)

Day 2: Examining the Mind

Practice: For fifteen minutes, whenever a thought or feeling arises, gently ask 'Who is thinking this?' or 'Who is feeling this?' Don't settle for the conceptual answer, 'I am,' but look directly for this 'I' that seems to be at the centre of experience. Is it in the head? The chest? Is it constant or changing? Does it have a shape or location?

Quote: 'The Buddha did not teach "no-self" as a doctrine to believe, but as a tool for examining our experience. When we look for a permanent, independent self, we cannot find one—only a collection of changing processes.' (Chapter 3)

Day 3: The Rainbow of Emptiness

Practice: For twenty minutes, contemplate the nature of a rainbow as a metaphor for emptiness. Visualise a rainbow appearing after a rainstorm—vividly present yet formed entirely through the relationships between sunlight, water droplets, and your perspective as the observer. If any of these elements were missing, the rainbow would not appear. Consider how the rainbow exists—neither as a solid, independent object, nor as a complete illusion, but as an appearance arising from causes and conditions.

Quote: 'The concept of emptiness doesn't mean things don't exist, but that they exist interdependently, without fixed, inherent existence. Like a rainbow that appears through the coming together of light, water, and an observer.' (Chapter 5)

Day 4: Perceptions and Reality

Practice: Choose an everyday object and examine it closely for ten minutes. First, observe how your mind automatically labels, categorises, and relates to it based on past associations. Then, try to see it freshly, as if encountering it for the first time. Observe the difference between the object as conceptualised and the raw sensory experience of colours, shapes, textures, and weight.

Quote: 'When we examine our perceptions closely, we discover something startling: rather than perceiving reality directly, we experience a mental construction shaped by our concepts, language, and past conditioning.' (Chapter 3)

Day 5: Interpretations and Experience

Practice: When facing a challenging situation today, pause and ask yourself: 'What is my interpretation of what's happening right now? Is this the only possible interpretation or could there be others?' Try adopting a different perspective, even briefly, and observe how this shift affects your emotional response and the range of actions available to you.

Quote: 'Our reactions to life events are shaped more by our interpretations than by the events themselves. By changing our perspective, we can transform our experience without changing external circumstances.' (Chapter 3)

Day 6: Beyond Concepts

Practice: Select a meaningful word or concept (like 'love', 'awareness', or 'freedom'). For fifteen minutes, work with it in three stages: First, reflect on the concept deeply—what does it mean? What experiences does it point to? Then, set aside the concept and try to experience directly what it points to beyond the label and definition. Finally, observe the difference between conceptual understanding and direct experience.

Quote: 'Concepts cannot capture ultimate reality. Yet we use concepts as tools to point toward that which is beyond conception, like using a thorn to remove a thorn before discarding both.' (Chapter 5)

Day 7: Integrating Wisdom and Compassion

Practice: For twenty minutes, explore the complementary nature of wisdom and compassion: Begin by contemplating impermanence and interdependence—how all phenomena, including yourself, arise depending on countless conditions and are constantly changing. From this space of wisdom, allow compassion to arise naturally. Recognising the shared vulnerability of all beings subject to impermanence, let your heart open to their struggles and aspirations.

Quote: 'Compassion without wisdom is incomplete, while wisdom without compassion remains sterile. These two qualities must be developed together, like the two wings of a bird needing each other for flight.' (Chapter 17)

4. Seven-Day Path: Finding Purpose and Meaning

Day 1: The Purpose of Life

Practice: For twenty minutes, contemplate the nature of genuine happiness: Sit quietly and reflect on what brings you genuine, lasting happiness rather than temporary pleasure. Consider the moments when you've felt most fulfilled and at peace. Observe what qualities were present—perhaps connection, meaning, generosity, clarity, or compassion.

Quote: 'The purpose of our lives is to be happy. It is not shallow, pleasure-based happiness, but deep satisfaction that comes from a compassionate heart and a clear mind. Each of us has the capacity and responsibility to create such meaningful happiness, not just for ourselves but for our world.' (Chapter 10)

Day 2: Pleasure Versus Happiness

Practice: Before making a choice meant to increase your happiness today—whether it's a purchase, an activity, or how to spend your free time—pause and ask yourself: 'Am I seeking pleasure or genuine happiness here? Will this choice leave me satisfied or wanting more?' Let this discernment guide your decisions, experimenting with choices that might lead to more lasting well-being.

Quote: 'There is an important distinction between pleasure and happiness. Pleasure is based primarily on physical sensations and is fleeting by nature. Genuine happiness is rooted in the mind—in inner peace, understanding, and compassion. True and lasting happiness comes from mental development and concern for others' welfare.' (Chapter 10)

Day 3: Warm-Heartedness

Practice: Begin today by setting an intention to approach everyone you meet with warm-heartedness. Imagine this quality as a warm light in your heart that you direct towards others. When you find yourself preoccupied with your own problems, try shifting attention to someone else's well-being—ask how they're doing with genuine interest, offer help with a small task, or simply send them good wishes silently.

Quote: 'The basic source of all happiness is a sense of kindness and warm-heartedness towards others. We are all the same as human beings; we all want happiness and not suffering. The moment you begin thinking about the welfare of others, your mind broadens and your own problems seem smaller.' (Chapter 10)

Day 4: Inner Development

Practice: Recall a time when external conditions were challenging, but an inner quality—like patience, courage, or compassion—helped you maintain stability and well-being. Observe how this internal resource supported you when external sources of happiness were unavailable. Then recall a time when external conditions were pleasant, but inner turmoil prevented you from enjoying them. Observe how inner states can override even favourable circumstances.

Quote: 'True happiness comes not from seeking pleasant experiences but from mental development—cultivating qualities like kindness, clarity, and wisdom that remain stable regardless of external circumstances.' (Chapter 10)

Day 5: Interdependent Well-being

Practice: Approach several interactions today with the question: 'How might I contribute to this person's happiness?' Observe whether focusing on others' happiness depletes your own or unexpectedly enhances it. At the day's end, reflect on whether prioritising mutual well-being led to more satisfaction than pursuing only your own interests would have.

Quote: 'If we neglect the welfare of others while pursuing our happiness, ultimately, we will fail in both aims. Our well-being is deeply connected to that of others. This is not idealism—it is a practical reality in our interconnected world.' (Chapter 10)

Day 6: Ethical Living

Practice: When making choices today, observe whether your motivation arises primarily from external rules, rational understanding, or intuitive wisdom. Without judging any level as better or worse, simply observe how different motivations feel and how they affect both your actions and your inner state.

Notice moments when ethical action arises naturally from clarity and care, requiring no internal debate or struggle.

Quote: 'When wisdom and compassion mature, ethical conduct becomes less about following rules and more a natural expression of our deepest understanding. We avoid harmful actions not from fear of consequences but from seeing their incompatibility with our true nature.' (Chapter 17)

Day 7: Beyond Self-Centredness

Practice: For twenty minutes, practise expanding your circle of concern: Begin by acknowledging your natural concern for your own well-being. Then, bring to mind someone you love deeply. Allow your care for their well-being to arise naturally, noticing how this concern feels in your heart. Gradually expand this circle to include acquaintances, strangers, and eventually all beings. With each expansion, repeat the phrase: 'Just as I wish to be happy and free from suffering, may they be happy and free from suffering.'

Quote: 'The essence of spiritual practice is to diminish self-centredness and expand our circle of concern. As we do this, we discover that our own happiness is intimately connected to the well-being of others.' (Chapter 10)

5. Seven-Day Path: The Journey of Transformation

Day 1: Beginning Where You Are

Practice: When you observe dissatisfaction with yourself today, pause to practise dual awareness: First, acknowledging your current reality with honesty and kindness, then connecting with your aspiration for growth. Observe how this balanced approach differs from both harsh self-judgement and complacent acceptance of limiting patterns.

Quote: 'Spiritual practice must begin with honest acceptance of our present condition—our strengths and limitations, our clarity and confusion. This truthful self-recognition, combined with genuine aspiration for growth, creates the proper foundation for the journey.' (Chapter 18)

Day 2: Balancing Effort and Patience

Practice: Observe your habitual tendency today in approaching challenges—do you typically lean towards impatient striving or passive acceptance? When you catch this tendency, experiment with bringing in the complementary quality: If you tend towards striving, introduce more patience and acceptance; if you tend towards passivity, bring in a clear intention and appropriate effort.

Quote: 'Inner transformation requires both diligent effort and patient acceptance. Too much striving creates tension and frustration, while too little effort leads to complacency. Finding the middle way between these extremes is itself a crucial practice.' (Chapter 18)

Day 3: Working with Obstacles

Practice: When encountering an obstacle today—whether external (a disruption, difficulty, or delay) or internal (resistance, confusion, or reactivity)—pause briefly to shift perspectives. Rather than seeing it merely as an unwelcome interference, ask: 'What might this teach me? What quality might it help me develop?' This slight shift transforms obstacles from mere hindrances to potential teachers.

Quote: 'Obstacles on the spiritual path—whether external difficulties or internal resistances—are not failures but opportunities for deeper learning. When approached with wisdom, these very challenges become catalysts for growth.' (Chapter 18)

Day 4: Recognising Progress

Practice: At the end of the day, rather than evaluating your practise based on how you felt or what experiences you had, observe one or two moments where your response to a situation reflected some quality you've been cultivating—perhaps a bit more patience, clarity, or compassion than would have been present in the past.

Quote: 'True spiritual progress often appears not in dramatic experiences but in subtle shifts in how we respond to daily situations. Decreasing reactivity, growing patience with difficulties, and greater concern for others' welfare are more reliable signs of transformation than temporary emotional states.' (Chapter 18)

Day 5: Continuous Unfolding

Practice: Observe when you fall into thinking of spiritual development as a linear progression towards a fixed endpoint today. When this happens, gently remind yourself of the continuous, spiral nature of the path. Consider one teaching or practice that has revealed different layers of meaning to you over time, appreciating how understanding continues to unfold rather than arriving at a final conclusion.

Quote: 'There is no final destination in spiritual development, no point where we can say "now I am complete". Rather, the path continues to unfold throughout our lives, with each stage revealing new dimensions of understanding and practice.' (Chapter 18)

Day 6: Inner and Outer Integration

Practice: Observe when you tend towards either extreme today—either withdrawing into inner experience at the expense of engagement or becoming so externally focused that you lose connection with your inner state. At these moments, practise rebalancing: If overly internal, extend awareness outwards to include others; if overly external, reconnect with your inner experience.

Quote: 'Inner development and social responsibility are not opposed but complementary. The deeper our inner transformation, the more effective our contribution to society becomes. And engagement with the world's challenges deepens our spiritual understanding.' (Chapter 17)

Day 7: Joy in the Journey

Practice: During one period of formal practice today, set aside all goal orientation and experience the practice as complete in itself—not a means to future attainment but the direct expression of awareness, wisdom, or compassion in this moment. Then extend this same perspective to one everyday activity, experiencing it not as a task to complete but as an opportunity to express mindful presence.

Quote: 'The journey of transformation is not merely a means to future happiness but contains its own joy in each step. When we recognise that each moment of practice is itself the expression of our Buddha nature, we discover happiness not as a distant goal but as inherent in the very process of awakening.' (Chapter 18)

Further Introductory Reading

The Art of Happiness: A Handbook for Living
His Holiness the Dalai Lama and Howard C. Cutler
A classic collaboration between the Dalai Lama and a Western psychiatrist, exploring how to find meaning and joy in everyday life through Buddhist principles applied to contemporary challenges.

Ethics for the New Millennium
His Holiness the Dalai Lama
A profound yet accessible exploration of how universal ethical principles can guide individuals and societies towards greater well-being, regardless of religious background.

The Universe in a Single Atom: The Convergence of Science and Spirituality
His Holiness the Dalai Lama
His Holiness examines the fascinating parallels between scientific inquiry and Buddhist contemplative investigation, offering a vision for how these approaches can complement each other.

Beyond Religion: Ethics for a Whole World
His Holiness the Dalai Lama
A compelling argument for a secular ethics based on our shared humanity and common values, accessible to people of all faiths and none.

How to Practice: The Way to a Meaningful Life
His Holiness the Dalai Lama, translated and edited by Jeffrey Hopkins
A practical, step-by-step guide to developing wisdom and compassion in daily life, with specific meditation practices and contemplations.

The World of Tibetan Buddhism: An Overview of Its Philosophy and Practice
His Holiness the Dalai Lama, translated and edited by Geshe Thupten Jinpa
A comprehensive guide to Tibetan Buddhist philosophy and practice from the tradition's foremost teacher, balancing depth with accessibility.

Stages of Meditation
His Holiness the Dalai Lama, translated by Geshe Lobsang Jordhen, Losang Choephel Ganchenpa, and Jeremy Russell
Based on the classic meditation manual by Kamalashila, this book offers detailed guidance on developing concentration and insight through progressive stages of practice.

Understanding the Dalai Lama
Rajiv Mehrotra
The essays in this volume shed light on the Dalai Lama's fascinating life, painting the portrait of a tireless champion of compassion, altruism, and peace.

His Holiness the Dalai Lama on Life, Living and Happiness
Rajiv Mehrotra
In this book, the Dalai Lama's messages of compassion, altruism, and peace are articulated in a unique secular ethic and supported with techniques and practices that can help one achieve these ideals.

In My Own Words
Rajiv Mehrotra
This is a fascinating collection of extracts from some of His Holiness's most powerful writings and talks. It brings together extracts from some of his most powerful writings and talks.

All You Ever Wanted to Know from His Holiness The Dalai Lama on Happiness, Love, Living & Much More
Rajiv Mehrotra
An edited compilation of mostly personal conversations spanning nearly twenty years between the Dalai Lama and Rajiv Mehrotra, one of his early disciples.

Destructive Emotions: How Can We Overcome Them?
Daniel Goleman (in conversation with the Dalai Lama)
Documents groundbreaking dialogues between the Dalai Lama, scientists, and contemplatives on understanding and transforming destructive emotions.

Altered Traits: Science Reveals How Meditation Changes Your Mind, Brain, and Body
Daniel Goleman and Richard J. Davidson
A rigorous scientific exploration of how meditation produces lasting positive changes in practitioners, written by two pioneers in contemplative neuroscience.

A Guide to the Bodhisattva Way of Life
Commentary by His Holiness the Dalai Lama on Shantideva's classic text
His Holiness's insightful commentary on this central text brings its ancient wisdom to life for contemporary practitioners.

Online Resources

Mind & Life Institute (www.mindandlife.org)
Founded in 1987 to foster dialogue between the Dalai Lama and scientists, this institute continues to advance the understanding of the mind and contemplative practices through research, publications, and events.

His Holiness the Dalai Lama's Official Website (www. dalailama.com)
Provides access to teachings, schedules, videos, and official statements from His Holiness.

The Foundation for Universal Responsibility of His Holiness the Dalai Lama (www.furhhdl.org)
Established with the Nobel Peace Prize awarded to His Holiness, this foundation supports projects embodying his vision of universal ethics, compassion, and peace.

This reading list is not exhaustive but offers a selection of resources for further exploration. Whether you're drawn to philosophical depth, scientific understanding, or practical application, these works provide reliable guidance for continuing the journey of wisdom and compassion.

Acknowledgements

IN COMPILING THIS BOOK, I HAVE DRAWN FROM YEARS OF serving His Holiness's teachings, his writings, and his laughter. I am not a scholar or spiritual authority—merely a sādhaka, an aspirant. Any errors or distortions are entirely my own. What I offer here is not a definitive interpretation but a heartfelt attempt to bridge the poetic and the practical—to share, as sincerely as I can, what I have tried to learn along this path.

It would not have been possible without the support and encouragement of my Tibetan family. I'm deeply grateful to Nagari Rinpoche and Rinchen Khando-la, who have been more than family to me for nearly fifty years. They have offered comfort, learning, and a sense of belonging throughout that time. I thank Tempa Tsering, Tenzin Geyche Tethong, and the late Lodi Gyari Rinpoche for their friendship and wise counsel. I'm also thankful to Tenzin Taklha, Chimmie Rinzing, and Tseten Choekyappa at the Private Office for their time and help despite the many demands on them. Thanks to Ashok Chopra of Hay House—publisher and friend—whose persistence and vision have helped bring this and many other books to life.

And to Meenakshi Gopinath, partner, companion, confidante, and fellow traveller—your unwavering presence is the rhythm beneath every word I write. It is your strength and insight that sustain me.

I offer my respect to the lineage of teachers, from the Buddha to the present day. This book is one small reflection of their enduring light.

May this book serve as a mirror for your heart, a lantern for your path, and a whispered thank-you to a teacher who has given us so much.

Do not dwell in the past, do not dream of the future, concentrate the mind on the present moment.

—BUDDHA